MARRIAGE

OF THE

MOON & JAGUAR

Part 2

FOREWARD

*A*t some point it seems everyone asks, *Who am I?* In the isolation of being human, the stories, and the myths have been rewritten to entertain the current tribal or societal paradigm. It's similar to the childhood game of 'telephone', where a story is passed from one to another by word of mouth. At the end, the group witnesses how a story can change in the manner or form it is told, with the final delivery of information quite tainted from the original tale. A simple story becomes more complex, a complex story over simplified. Imagine what happens when a story is told in metaphor or poetic lyrics?

Hence, the continuation of the Marriage of the Moon and Jaguar, Tome 3: The Lattice, germinated on it's own due to production limits and mostly, to provide a pause, breakpoint, in a wildly symbolic tale.

While many ideas are brought to the pages of this myth, I hope it encourages one to consider the depth and mystery of larger cycles. Patterns so large and confounding that quantum physics, single preference religions, government, or mass media rarely reveal the range of possibilities with a viable amount of curiosity and wonder. If we eliminated attachment and ego from our weaving of creation stories, we might get a more entertaining, authentic representation of a vast and incredibly dense story.

How we got here is the same as a star. Look up. What we will become is like a tree when a seed is planted. The DNA forms from chapter 1, we are all divine co-creators, co-evolving spinning of new branches in the tree of live into a myriad of forms. Only that kernel of light actually knows anything of itself, and yet, even its holographic projection continues in the moment to bend with various influences.

As we continue on the dramatic evolution of Lolaboy, I'd like you to consider less about the syntax and exact interpretation of the conjoined words, and spend more time opening your heart and mind to the limitless, effortless wonder of existence. Live. Create. Wonder.

Now, part 2 of the Marriage of the Moon & Jaguar, The Lattice… invites you into…the unknown….

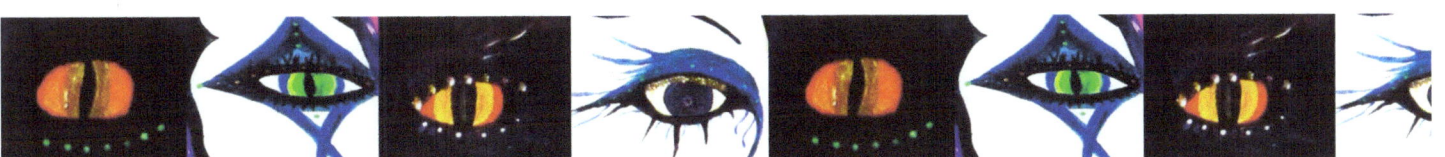

We speak of Time and Mind, which do not
easily yield to categories. We separate
past and future and find that Time is an
amalgam of both. We separate good and evil
and find that Mind is an amalgam of both.
To understand, we must grasp the whole.
—Isaac Asimov

In futurity I prophetic see,
that the earth from sleep
(grave the sentence deep)
shall arise, and seek
for her maker meek
and the desert wild
become a garden wild.
—William Blake

The times require
that every one
should speak out boldly:
...every man should do his duty
in Arts, as well as in Arms,
or in the Senate.
—William Blake

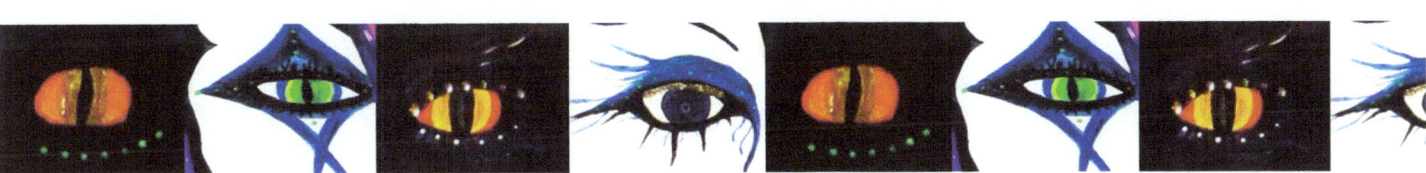

TOME 3

THE LATTICE

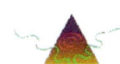

So far, Lolaboy's pilgrimage had intricately encouraged heshe's navigational skills, to develop and increase their abilities of how to maintain an infinite number of responses to challenges. Ocelotl, Serpiente Pluma and DreamWeaver gathered in great counsel with the Creators at a distant outpost in the galactic vortex.

"Welcome masters of the matrix, we advise you that the final descent of the plumed serpent begins shortly and the alignment of the astrophysical pathways has been set into motion." The Creators continued, "While the navigational skills are paramount for traversing the depths of consciousness, proficiency of willingness is necessary to align with heart-knowing they shall grant the pathways to open within the dynamic center of all time... We suggest that your team integrate deeper practice on repair tactics. The consciousness lattice quivers under the pressure and threatens to break apart the critical density of the holografica field within Gaia's realm."

Ocelotl stood up and offered, "We understand great keepers of this complex story. Soon we will guide our players into a multi-layered sequence of events that promote further attention and focus on the vibrant webbing for manifesting light forms. We seek your guidance on matters that deter the attachment of inorganica and sinisteros to members of our group."

The atmosphere vibrated around the counsel and several images began to form. Several quasaria and orbic structures flashed into the darkness. At the center of the spiral galaxia a channel of light reflected into its feathered arms. Rows of lines and shapes produced a giant schema with several points blinking and radiating various colors. Harmonic tones arced, melodies blended tinny sounds with deep resonant bellows.

"We invite you to explore the initiate series of the integral primal lattice which shapes possibilities and tendencies for holografica fields to respond and interact. It is here some of you must focus your will and persuade its energetic response. This will help to wield its way onto a track that combines the negative and positive charges of the affected world. Then, the force that you mention will resolve and the polarization sequences will charge the matrices to integrate the most excellent potential outcome." The mysterious collaboration of counsel of Creators vaporized.

Ocelotl took a deep sigh. "At times, nothing makes sense they say. What do you think Serpiente Pluma? DreamWeaver?"

"As it is a fantastical dominion where ideas and desires formulate consequence, then I presume that the Creators just invited us to dive deeper into the structure of code modification and support us by incorporating additional tangible practice of authentic magic," stated DreamWeaver.

"Sssssssooooo myssssteriousssssly and poignantly offered dear iguana. However, while the densssssity of layersssss with riddles and metaforica were proffered by the Creatorsssss, complex asss it issss to imbibe, by mere ssssssuggessssstion, are we not willing to allow sssssynchronisssity and wonder to further thissssss perplexing ssssstory?" Serpiente Pluma continued, "Lo, Ocelotl, they referred to the desssscent of the sssserpent..."

Tremors quaked the atmosphere.

"Nonetheless, allies, I believe that Lolaboy's quest is about to dive deeper into the methods of actual conjuring and magic-at-will, thus assisting our mission. Can we agree on that and return to the solaria sistem? That quivering suggests that something has indeed spawned and there is profound change occurring more rapidly than I had deemed. Together, then?" Ocelotl joined arms with his comrades and they spun themselves into the universo closer to the realm of Gaia.

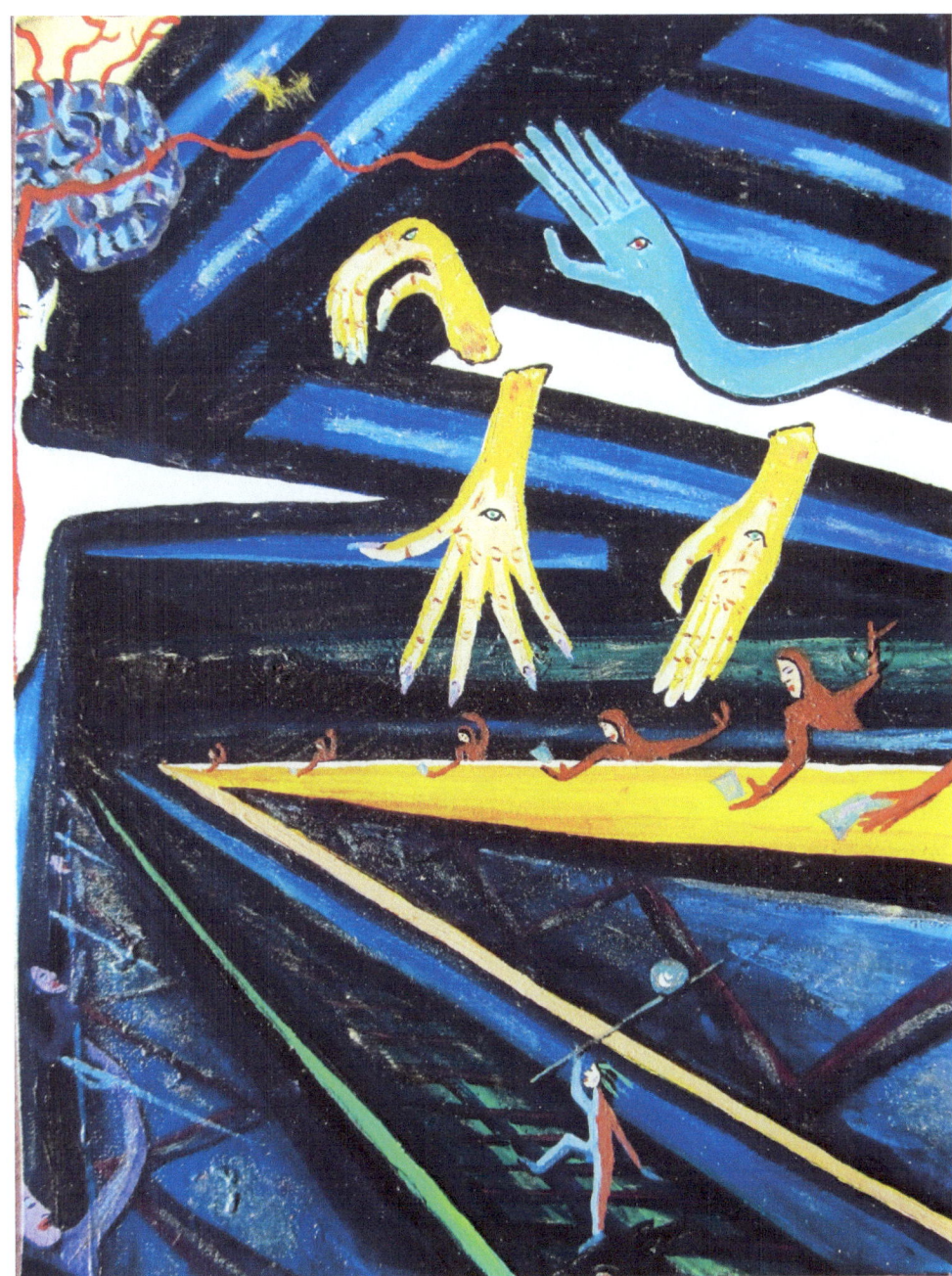

Quite strangely, off in the distance, Lolaboy sighted the dazzling entrance for the Carnival of Souls. Relieved somewhat, heshe was delighted to find a point of reference again. The journey had so many twists and turns it was hard to tell where heshe was at any given time.

On the edge of the Urban Jungle Lola saw a curved road that seemed to span indefinitely into the horizon. Banked on either side were a number of three story buildings. Their concrete facades formed a cavernous boulevard. Heshe turned to their side. There was a sign post that read, *Memoria Lane.*

Lola carried a magical pack on a stick, which was slumbered over heshe's shoulder. In it was the bottle of juice they had grabbed before leaving the forest just in case of thirst. Lolaboy popped open the glass bottle and sipped. The liquid refreshed heshe's energy. Lola had a gut feeling that a sip of the elixir would be needed to traverse this next leg in the journey.

Lolaboy marched forth gleefully onto the thoroughfare. Hanging from windows to either side were several humanos. They waved gayly at Lolaboy. To the right they extended hands and offered heshe perfectly square mirrors. From the left were purple-faced humanos whom offered heshe gleaming swords. While the offerings were interesting, Lolaboy's attention was drawn to a large white man with blue pants at the end of the lane. It had been a while since heshe had been at a gate, so Lolaboy decided to ask the question again, "*Who am I?*" Heshe's words reverberated and bounced from the surrounding buildings, and echoed so forcefully they nearly knocked Lola onto the ground.

All of a sudden, the road changed into a great metallic hallway. Then something very weird happened. A few white gloved hands dropped from the ceiling. Perplexed, Lolaboy wondered, what do these beings want from me?

"Aha! This is The Path of Innocence. Although, it can also be referred to as the avenue that directs one towards a new myth. If you have erased all time and no time successfully these routes together shall put you at the Gate to Judgementa or Trusta," blatantly stated the large white man. He continued to walk to the end of haunting corridor.

"What did you say?" Lolaboy was confused. All at once, it seemed everything in the hallway tried to coerce the young jaguar everyone competed for the magician's attention. Lola curled up and leaned against a wall like a frightened mouse.

"Of course, we have the truth Sayers, activators of the opocolyptus, and there are the Golden Octavia Reflectoras. Do you prefer to spend time with the complements, or the mirrors," asked the stark man? He seemed to get larger by the moment.

"I don't *know*!" Lolaboy scrunched heshe's brow. Heshe watched as terrifying hands snatched at the jaguar from every direction.

"In this hall are all the memorias, past, presente, futura of the regiona de humanos and the universo divino. I am Mondaminda the One Who Constructs Reality," paused the man. Then he added, "I *think* I am anyway… who knows?

Here in this corridor you deconstruct the current mythos. If you desire, then everything is eeeeerased, eeeeradicated and reeeevised. Now, to the left, we have the *categories*. This, that, not quite, possible yes, definitely of course, maybe, doubtful, or YES! Isn't the mind a wonderful place?" Mondaminda chortled and guffawed so loud the entire hall shattered into pieces...

Lolaboy abruptly started to spin and rotate in ever decreasing circular formations. It was similar to the feeling heshe had from the story petals Ocelotl had given them a long time ago. Heshe swirled and fell into a chasm that had opened in the hallway. The gaping hole opened wider at a maddening pace while the hall collapsed upon itself. Lolaboy plummeted into the gulf of darkness below…

"*It* is not the *I* that makes the self! It is not the *I* that makes the self," mumbled Lolaboy as heshe whirled in space. Where was heshe going now? Lolaboy plunged faster and faster until, with a loud thump, heshe hit solid ground. The atmosphere cleared and Lolaboy found themselves on the edge of what looked like a giant fabrica. Some sort of industrial unit sputtered and churned out tiny little cerebros. The brainos quickly spurted out from every direction. They lurched up rubber conveyor belts, then down a channel and into a chute.

"Next." Ca thump. "Next." Cathump. A monotonous voice bellowed from a loudspeaker in a corner of the room. The area was filled with blazing white neon light. In the center of the space was a blood red whirlpool.

The droning voice continued. "Next. Add some apathy! Hurry now, futility needed here! Next! Next! Next!"

Lolaboy hesitatingly peered into the core of the whirlpool. Heshe felt unusually magnetized toward the spiraling current. It pulled Lola closer and closer. Mesmerized, heshe jumped down to take a glimpse of what was inside the strange, swirling nucleus.

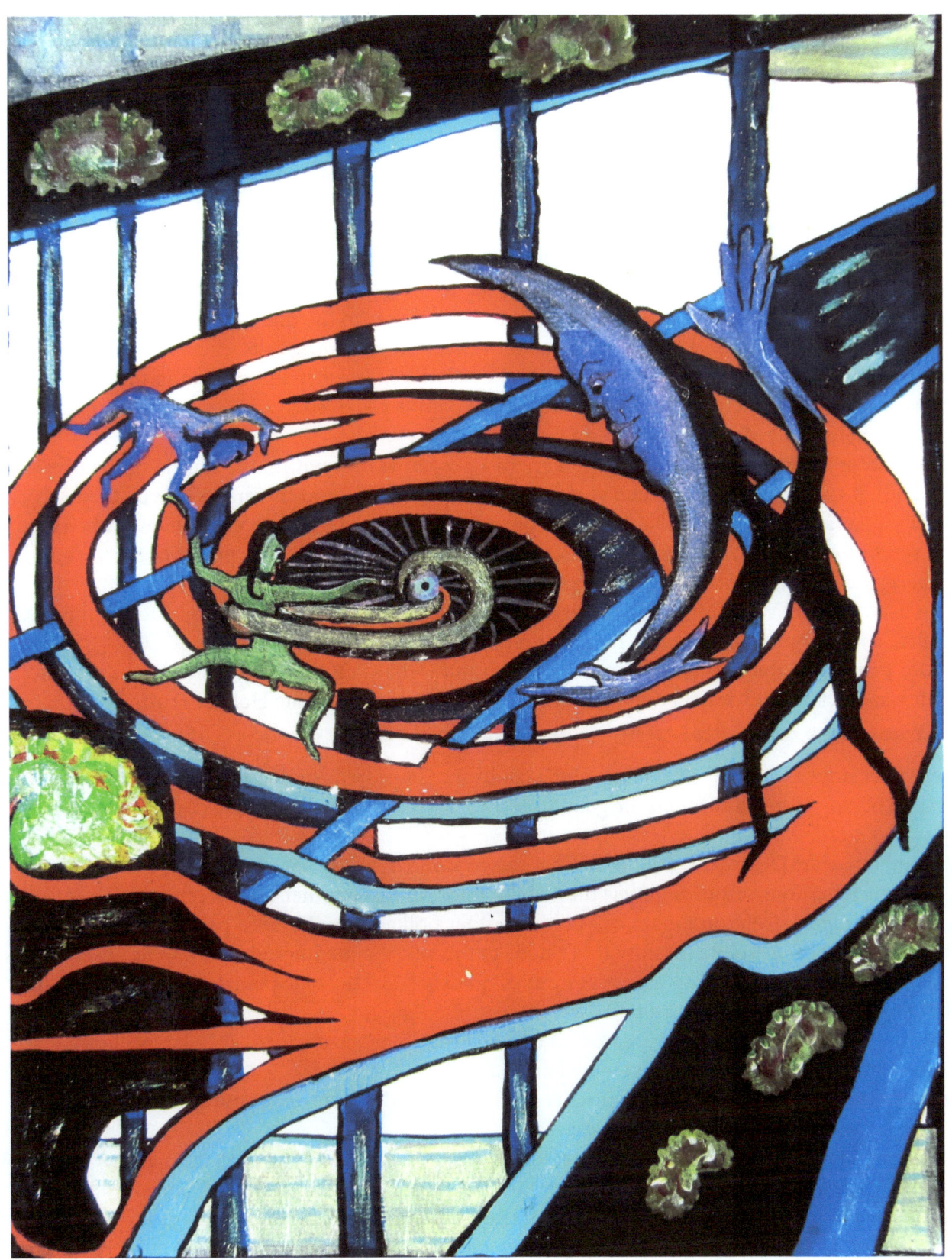

"You must look like this in order to succeed! The *rules*! 5099 says you shouldn't *ever*, never, never **ever** do THAT! Here. Take this deluded pattern and try it on," said a droning voice.

Without thinking, Lolaboy stepped onto the outer edges of the whirlpool. A path formed that led to the center. Heshe felt lured like a vacuum, almost sucked uncontrollably into the unknown vortex. Lolaboy heard voices from inside the frightening abyss.

"Heeeelp us! Heeeeeeelp ussssss! We are the other jaguar magicians… heeeelp us… please… We don't want to be a part of zombilandia … Come save us… Protect us…," screeched the voices that echoed throughout the enormous chamber.

Heshe's heart pulsed and tremored. I must do something! Perhaps I can dive in there and pull them out? *Finally*, my quest! "I will SAVE them! I am the ONE! Wait for me!"

Lolaboy raced around the red spiral, closer and closer to the gaping center until suddenly the force of the vacuum could no longer be resisted. Heshe was sucked ever nearer to the massive hole. There's no hope… I **must** save them, heshe thought. Lola could no longer resist their alarming calls.

Lolaboy's actions reverberated into the divino universo which urgently summoned in the ethers and cast a counter response. Immediately, on the blood hued spiral pathway arrived a familiar, curved silhouette. Then, emerging from behind, another shape materialized!

"Lolaboy! Stop! Turn back! It's a trick! You are in a perpetual hole within the Matrix of the Mind. Grab onto my hand! It's me, Morgano, and Luna Oscuro!" The divine twin and the moon heaved themselves towards the jaguar magician and pulled Lolaboy's outstretched arm. Terrifying winds blew and swirled. The strong currents blocked heshe's friends dramatic attempt to deflect the immense power of the vortex. The force of energy fiercely tore Lolaboy from the grasp of Morgano and Luna Oscuro.

"It's no use… We HAVE HIM NOW!" shrieked a voice. "Heshe's filled with apathy, futility, there's no use! Bahahahaha! Into our pit of darkness… the madness of the restless mind…"

Thunder penetrated the chasm and shook Morgano and Oscuro off their feet which broke their hold on Lolaboy. It was too late, they watched in vain as Lolaboy was sucked into the Hole of Truth…

***

There were lines and grids for as far as heshe could see. Hundreds of them crisscrossed and formed a giant mesh. Lolaboy plopped through the giant hole into the place known as Betwixt, or the place between worlds.

"Oh dear. Oh dear! Dear, dear! Oh *dear*. What can be done now," fussed someone in a polka dot uniform?

"Stop the ruckus. Your responsibility is the Grid! Quick, there's another hole over there! If we don't stop the leak it will change perception too much," urged another polka dot uniformed person!

"Madness… this is! Absolute insanity… We need to thicken the membrane here, too much energy is being lost. The zombias are sucking the energy out so quickly from the blue planeta it's disintegrating... Oh dear, what do we *do*," screamed a third polka dotted being?

Just then, an enormous creatura appeared. It towered over and gazed down at Lolaboy's body which had just emerged from a hole. Heshe seemed to be barely alive.

"Banzeb! Oh Keeper of the Matrices, Teacher of Teachers and the entire harmonics There are holes in Betwixt everywhere," shouted the polka dot creaturas!

A deafening sigh came from the giant being. Benzab roared, "Change your thoughts gridworkers!" The red ochre giant started to hum deep bass tones and then changed to higher pitched whines. With every note, the holes in the matrix began to repair themselves. The winds calmed down. The commotion ceased.

Lolaboy began to stir and opened their bloodshot eyes. The three gridworkers, as they were referred to, gathered around the hole and watched the jaguar.

"Wake up little one. It's us again. The Jaguar Diva Queens? Remember us?" One of the polka dot

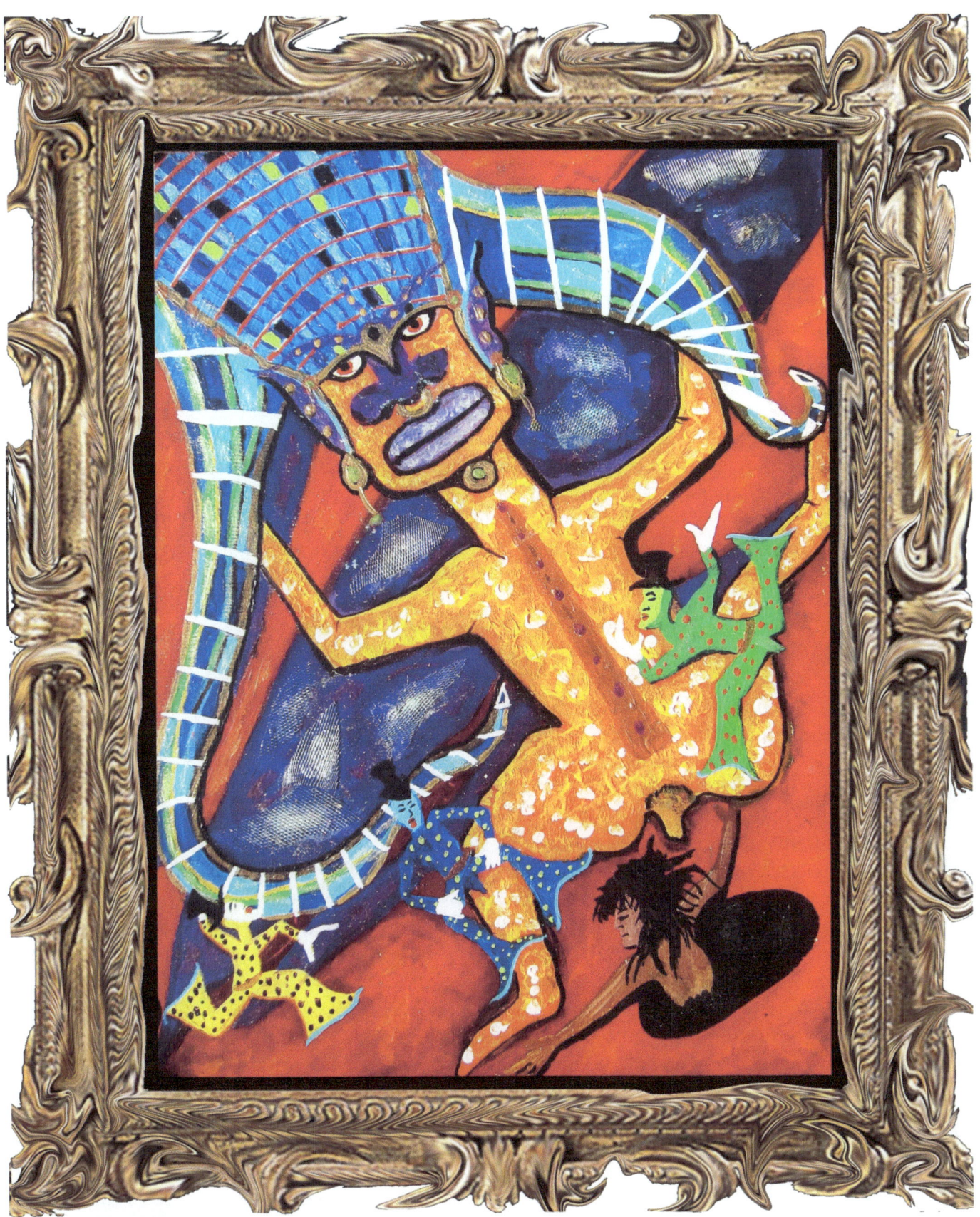

outfitted shemons lifted Lolaboy up from the gap in the ground.

"W…ww… where am I? Whaaa…wuuuu…what has happened," murmured Lolaboy?

Banzeb spoke, "Jaguar. This is the hole between worlds. You have now had a taste of time travel", chuckled the teacher. "This is the Universal Time Matrix. Someone must have transposed and though you here, because I wonder if you are actually capable of biolocation yet. However here you are! This is where the harmonies of the universo come together and form positions and reflective fields."

"um… ok…", muttered Lolaboy. "But why am I here? I thought I was going to help the others, the jaguar magicians, I could hear them crying… they need me…" Lolaboy remembered the whirlpool. "Wait. I remember something else… Oscuro and Morgano? They were there too?"

"They are fine. Luna Blanca actually came to your rescue during that dastardly trick of the mind. The others had lost their hold. Whether you are actually needed here, or not, is relative to what you are *compelling* with your free will in the universo…

It could be the result of entering the opposing fields of right or wrong. However, neither exists here. Here one can absorb the discipline of Neutrality Consciousness. Somehow, you have activated your twin consciousness matrix or what some refer to as Core Essencia."

"Luna Blanca? I didn't see her. Was she there too?" Lola paused. "Ok…I get *part* of this… so my thoughts were all over the place. But how were my friends called upon to help?"

"The ego has profound ways of interacting with the psyche and can, at times, beneficially send messages into the ethers. However, listen to me Lolaboy, I'll offer more guidance on the matrices soon; I think for now, it's wise you finish *this* leg of your journey before you learn anything else… before any *other* mischief can happen. Luna Blanca awaits you. She wants you to gather an item from your future self."

Benzab hummed three deep vibrating tones that penetrated deep into Lolaboy's mind. Once again heshe was plunged into darkness.

*C*ircus music softly played in the strange calmness. The ground beneath Lolaboy was rocky and cool. Surrounding the young magician was a deep, dark, pine forest; the evergreens towered hundreds of feet above Lola. Normally, Lola was acquainted with the identity of majestic allies such as these, however, heshe was not familiar with the names of these trees. Lolaboy rubbed their bloodshot eyes from what seemed days of interrupted rest. Heshe peered around the conifer grove and sharpened their focus. Past a thicket of trees, sloping down a large mountain were twinkling lights that steadily buzzed from inside the Carnival of Souls and Circo de Duendes. Down the left side of the hill was a bright lavender, vaguely familiar pyramid. Could it be the Pyramid of Remembrance, Lolaboy wondered? Why had it changed color? Heshe shuddered.

The young magician was perched on a stony cliff. Just below, the sea crashed onto a cluster of jagged rocks. Heshe noticed several subtle changes. Lolaboy gazed in confusion at the appearance of appendages on heshe's body. They were dramatically different. Long muscular limbs had now changed into thin, leathery arms. Once taut dark skin was now tough and coarse. Lola pulled a few hairs from their scalp. They were no longer jet black, but a mixture of grey, silver and white. It was as if heshe had aged *suddenly*—and rapidly. What had Benzab said about bioloca… something or other… or time travel?

Well if this was the future, why were so many things still the same? Heshe stood up and examined the horizon. What am I supposed to do *here*, heshe wondered? Maybe I'm supposed to head back towards the circo? But it looked far away… and there was a deep valley separating them.

Then, Lolaboy's heart warmed, for off in the distance, the dull light of the rising moon could be seen. Luna was coming; maybe she would help? In the meantime, I'll wait here in silence and take in the lessons from the past gates and mirrors.

First, there had been the mirrors that Luna had offered and then the strange branches that offered guidance, from Sikey, Spiri and Mistik. Indeed, some of the gates had changed the way Lolaboy mused

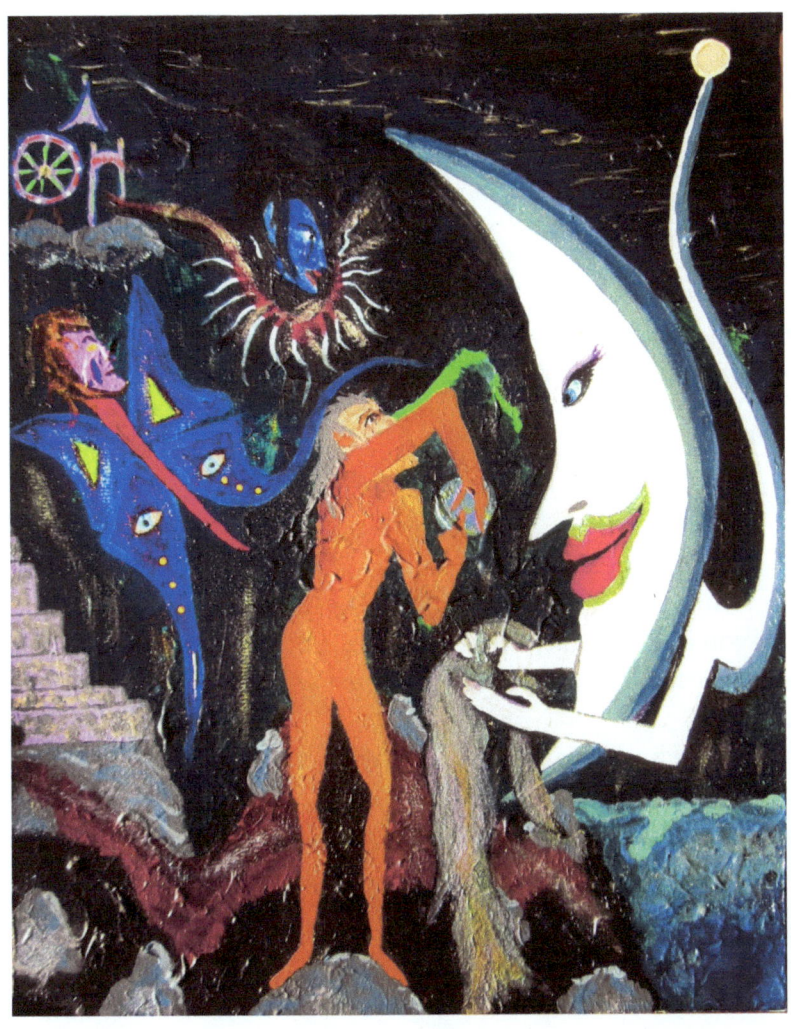

while others had deeply challenged and at times confused the direction of the quest. Yet, there in the distance was the gate, which Lola remembered as the entrance to the Circo Duendes; it was where Lola had entered the voyage of the self.

Then there was the Keeper of the Masks, and the key… the KEY! Lolaboy reached inside heshe's pocket and touched the key. Well… I don't see any door or window, or mirror or anything of the sort… Still, Lolaboy rubbed intently on the curvy metal form in their hand and focused on a door.

"Weeeelll done," came a voice from to heshe's side. A glorious butterfly spread bright blue wings and flapped toward Lolaboy.

"Metamor," queried Lola. Was this the butterfly genie? It resembled their friend, but was somewhat different. Its eyes were empty of life.

"Uh, not exactly, I am the *remembrance* of Metamor. I am Transformata, a new version of your dear friend. Good of you to bring out the key though, it has awakened the energy of possibility around you." The butterfly genie came to rest on a rock near Lolaboy.

Off in the distance, the weird and wonderful face that had welcomed Lola to the Carnival of Souls stretched itself and reached across the entire valley until it was almost in front of the rock where Lolaboy sat. For a moment, it was like Lolaboy had never left the entrance of the Carnival. The creaking of large cranks maneuvered the eerie clown like visage and soon after its mouth as it had before, opened.

"Welcome to the future-now." The voiced rattled off words. "Behind. You. Is the… Sea of Consiousness. In there you may retrieve something useful to your ancient future past." The mouth shut with a loud rusty clank.

By now the moon had risen. It was just above the edge of the Sea of Consciousness. What a lovely place, it no longer seemed strange about the changes on heshe's body. In general, Lolaboy *felt* the same.

"Lolaboy! I've got a gift for you!" The moon dropped from the sky until it hovered in front of the jaguar magician.

"Why, Luna Blanca, there's no need for gifts… I am fine and feel like I have everything I need," exclaimed Lolaboy.

"That is good news to hear, yet, still, here… take these." Luna held out stunning opalescent garments. "These are the Robes of Protection. Many of us feel that you have a few unwanted entities that have become attached to your purpose. The elevated consciousness of which you quest has attracted a number of observers and potential bvampirian leeches." Luna Blanca continued, "This ability you have to travel, advanced through your encounter with Benzab, enabled you to receive this gift. Normally it is something acquired through the passing of time, or aging as the humanos call it, a rite of passage, however, we believe

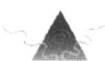

you have crossed this initiation early and there for we now offer them to you."

Lolaboy put on the robes. Shortly afterward, something shifted in heshe's entire presence… a deep knowing, a pivotal new sense of understanding. "Thank you, I will wear them well."

"Lolaboy, there is one *other* thing. By traveling to your future self, known the as an abuelo identity matrix, you now have other new abilities. Try rubbing your hands together and think of a heart's desire, but something tangible, like an apple. See what happens." Luna watched as the jaguar magician waved their hands into the air.

Heshe had focused on the Phoenix, the grand bird that had carried Lola throughout their childhood. Lola conjured the thought and directed it towards heshe's hands…suddenly a strange feeling came from heshe's backside. A tickling sensation and then…could it be? How strange! Lolaboy had imagined the grande bird and now… heshe twisted around and saw large iridescent bluish-white wings had sprouted from their back!

"Well, my goodness! What an amazing ability you have! Indeed, wings," beamed Luna Blanca! "What were you thinking of my friend?"

"Of the Phoenix," grinned Lolaboy.

"To be sure! Now there you are! However, at this point, Lolaboy, I must advise you that no one should stay too long in another time zone other than the one you are currently attending too. Of course you arrived here for important endowments to assist you on the *adventurer's quest*, however, I must send you back in time and space, to where you were in the here and now…"

Without hesitation, Lolaboy felt a sensation of rising, up and up and up, heshe was flying! Into the unknown they flew.

*L*olaboy stationed in darkness for a moment. Then, suddenly beneath them appeared startling long staircase which seemed to go off into the horizon for eternity. While Lola flew around in space, another bird flew up to heshe and hovered parallel to the jaguar magician.

"Wise magician you are! Quite the flight you have taken! It's me, Night Messenger." The mystifying owl that had initiated Lola, alongside Ocelotl when heshe was a young magician, was now flying next to them. "If you want, we can take a rest. Fly with me. I'll meet you on those stairs below."

"Right, then, I will." Lolaboy was new at flying; it felt great but was certainly an awkward feeling at times. Lola landed gracefully, like a seasoned swan, onto one of the steps in the impressive spiral staircase. Lola gently folded the large wings upon their back. The jaguar noticed that an intricate mesh actually formed the steps. A geometric pattern folded upon itself over and over, the steps climbed up to a series of sapphire gates.

"Where am I," asked Lolaboy?

"Why dear one, you are on the steps which lead from the place of time-no-time to time immortal. These very steps weave the patternas of *ah Day eN A*. Remember what Sera Pheam had offered to you at the Gate of Release and Attachment? These codigos hold the entirety of evulvolooshon. This is the Path of Ascensionata and each of these gates contributes to the matrix of possibility. There are four gates. Be-leaf. Discriminata. Unit-tee. And the last is Trustica."

Lolaboy felt something vibrate near their right side. Heshe gazed down at a cluster of moaning life forms. While they bared a resemblance to humanos, none of them had eyes. They had an overall emptiness as well. "What are they," asked Lolaboy pointing to the forms?

"Zombias. Unfortunately they have dislodged and dislocated their consecutive weave of codigos in *ah Day eN A*." Night Messenger paused, then reflected, "Remember the story flowers that Ocelotl and I introduced you too? Each one of these steps, are similar, in that, they contain an integral part of the collective evulvolooshon of humanos, the developing story of all *vida* or life on the Planet of Great Consciousness.

Throughout this staircase are scattered a total of twelve gates to master. You may have to refine them later, but for now, sense that magic at foot."

"Wow, that seems like a lot, or at least a *long* way to go." Lolaboy felt a welling up of disappointment.

"Ah, their reflekshon is strong on you." The Owl motioned to the Zombias. "Here, take this." Night Messenger handed a brilliant gold shield to Lolaboy. "This is a cover referred to as the *Guardis of Interdependencia*. It can help protect you from the disadvantageous whims of woe-be-gones."

"Thank you. I have so many new gifts and abilities. Although, I wonder of my aptitude to use them well." Lolaboy held the shield high in the air and admired its refined etchings.

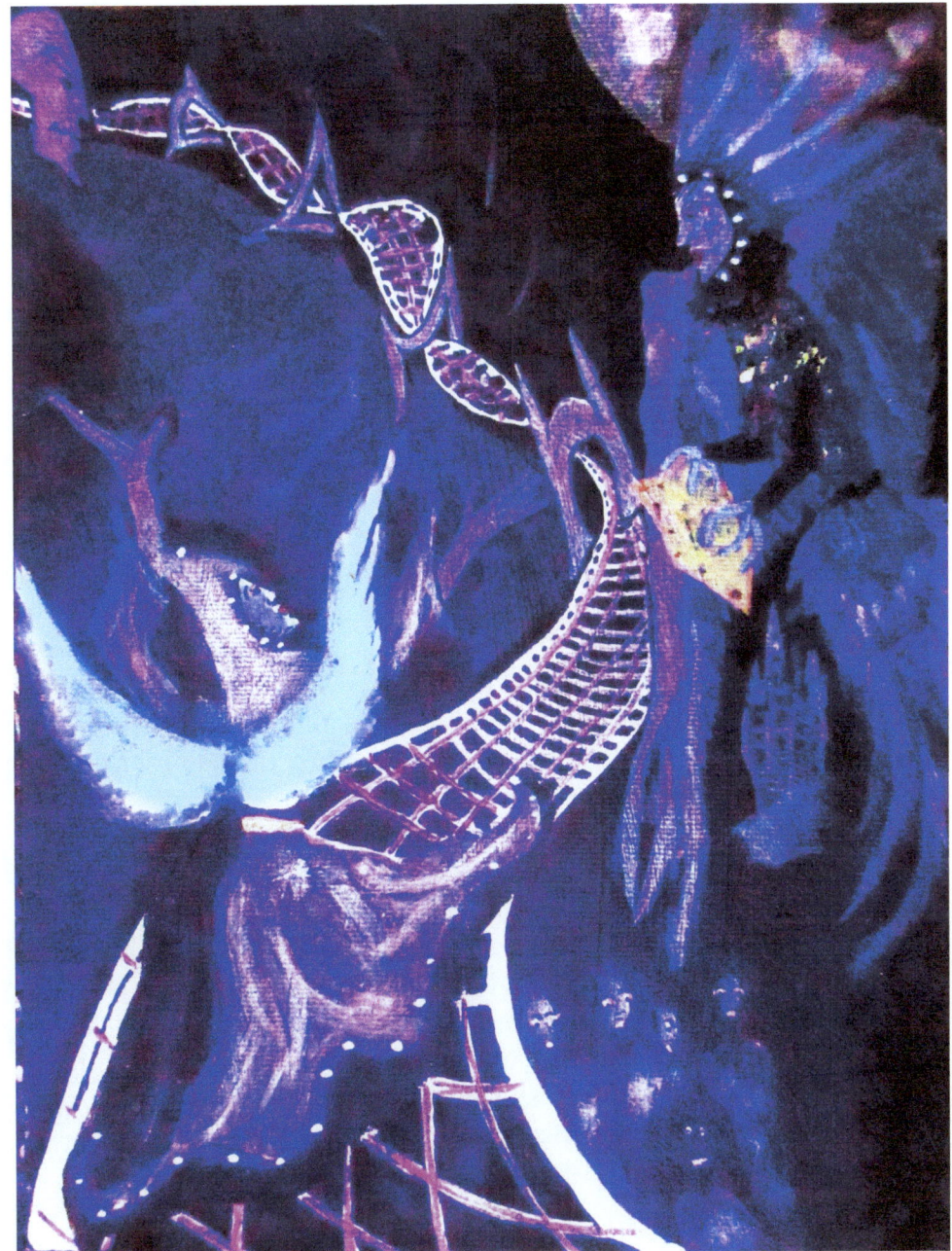

"Ah my plumed jaguar, you will have time enough to perfect the use to be sure. After the next four gates, you shall pass one more time through a tricky passage of muerte or mortality. From there you will be invited to go through the *Looking Glass of RezArekshon*." Night Messenger observed as another visitor came from the distance. It was Luna Oscuro.

"Greetings Lola, how magnificent. You've gained angelic plumage to soar with!" Luna Oscuro dimly glowed on the horizon.

"Dear Luna! So much time has passed since our last meeting."

"To be sure, much has happened to you! Nevertheless, my ally, this shield… Night Messenger, did you explain clearly its intended use to Lolaboy?"

"Mostly." The owla turned to Lolaboy. "It is to aid you in deflecting the angra or feelings of unfairness you may come to witness on the Planet of Great Consciousness. You have arrived from a more harmonic environ, La Selva, where justice is the foundation of all things. However, as of late, the planeta is a place of disequilibrio. Unfortunately, the realm of Gaia, has succumbed to unreasonable acts of judgment and malicious verdicts."

Luna Oscuro approached his two friends. "Dear jaguar, you are now called forth to a new place. I think

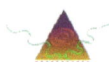

it is a period and location where you will experience a bit more ease and tranquility—at *least* for a time." The moon turned to Night Messenger and frowned while hiding his expression from Lola. "For the Planet of Great Consciousness it is a time of learning new ways to communicate. We would like to introduce you to a language that we hope will be helpful for the time when you return onto the tiny blue planet."

"Very well," ascertained Lolaboy. "Now, I will continue upon my quest with more fervor. I'm ready to climb these steps and… one," up heshe climbed, "two… three… I believe. I trust. I Unify. I set off…upon the final legs of my quest!" Lola waved goodbye to heshe's friends and marched up the eternal path.

In reality it seemed to take no time at all to get through the gates. Each door bestowed Lolaboy with a delicate but significant increase in their sense of determination and willingness. Heshe marched up the steps and through the Looking Glass of RezArekshon with no relapse into fear or the temptation of pandamonia. Once through the looking glass, heshe stepped into an immense mossy meadow. Luscious, vibrant vegetation spread for as far as one could see; in the center was a large serene, crystal blue lake, so clear that ruby and cobalt colored rocks could be seen beneath the surface. Majestic purple mountains towered next to the lake, abruptly rising from the western edge like mammoth sized teeth. Near the water's rim stood an amber pagoda hut. Lolaboy decided to go there and take a rest while contemplating the journey.

Once inside, Lola found several books and a small urn with twigs. Lolaboy looked at the sticks and longed for a fire to warm heshe's weary bones after an exceptionally long expedition. At once, small flames ignited the wood and a fire soothed Lolaboy's fragile nerves. Reminded of the power of thought, Lola made a decision to be careful with their desires.

Lola picked up a thickly bound, gilded book and skimmed through the first few worn, yellowed pages. To be sure, heshe detected it was some sort of ancient manuscript and everything about it peaked Lola's curiosity. In it were details of how humanos were actually liquid light bodies. They were holografica reflekshons and masques of the ego.

Lolaboy continued to peruse its content. Heshe came to realize some of the text nearly described the exact journey they had just taken! The book had hundreds of elaborate diagrams: it showed that there was a meaning for each number. 1=unity. 2=dualidad, 3 rhythm, 4 order, 5 center, 6 balancia and receptivity, and finally, 7, it proclaimed that it represented mystic woo.

There was also a map. It was a chart that plotted the entire surrounding area. The body of water was called the Lake of Reflekshon. The map referred to rivers which flowed into the lake. One of them flowed from the west; it was identified as the River of Recolekshon. The other was referred to as the River of Absentmindedness. What funny names, thought Lolaboy. Heshe continued to discover other areas on the chart. There were the mountains called the Peaks of Possibilities. The entire region was referred to as the Place of Contemplashon. Wow, what a space to land, mused Lolaboy! Luna Oscura had been correct!

Lolaboy felt fatigued and wanted to lie down and dream a bit. From the other side of the lake one of the mountains rumbled. A thin orange glow appeared from the top of a peak. Above it, heshe saw a few stars twinkling. Each had seven points. Shallow waves crossed the surface of the lake, their splashes hummed as they hit the shore, soothing Lolaboy with a sweet lullaby. Heshe quickly fell asleep.

Heshe dreamed deeply throughout the night. In a vision, Lola was traveling backwards through the *adventurer's quest*. Seemingly, heshe returned and passed through each of the gates, each of mirrors until once again, they went back in la Selva. There, beneath a tree Lola saw an elaborately decorated book. Covered with golden script, it was titled, *The Sacrificed Myths of Forgotten Times: The Cosmic Mysteries*. Heshe walked over and picked up the tome. While gleaning parts of the first chapter, heshe discovered that there had been seven-pointed master artisan stars which had seeded humanos with creativity. It mentioned how the humanos had once been benevolent, magically potent and gentle beings. It also stated, that there had been a great separation, a rift in the cosmic web. Afterwards humanos were, to some extent, cut off from their divine wholeness and their connection to everything that was exquisitely genuine. It was the falling from truth. The manuscript offered that many avatars had descended to the blue planeta and offered realignment to limitless possibilities. Yet, their original intent was continuously distorted, leaving humanos inherently stuck in a repetitive growth cycle on their evolushun. Strangely, after reading that part, the book vanished in heshe's hands and the dream faded.

While Lolaboy had been sleeping, a visitor had arrived to the lake. It was La Cougera, the Moon Jaguar, a distant cousin to Ocelotl. This was her realm, the Territory of Intuition and Process, Empathy and Synchronicity. She had been patiently waiting for the young jaguar to arrive. She observed Lolaboy

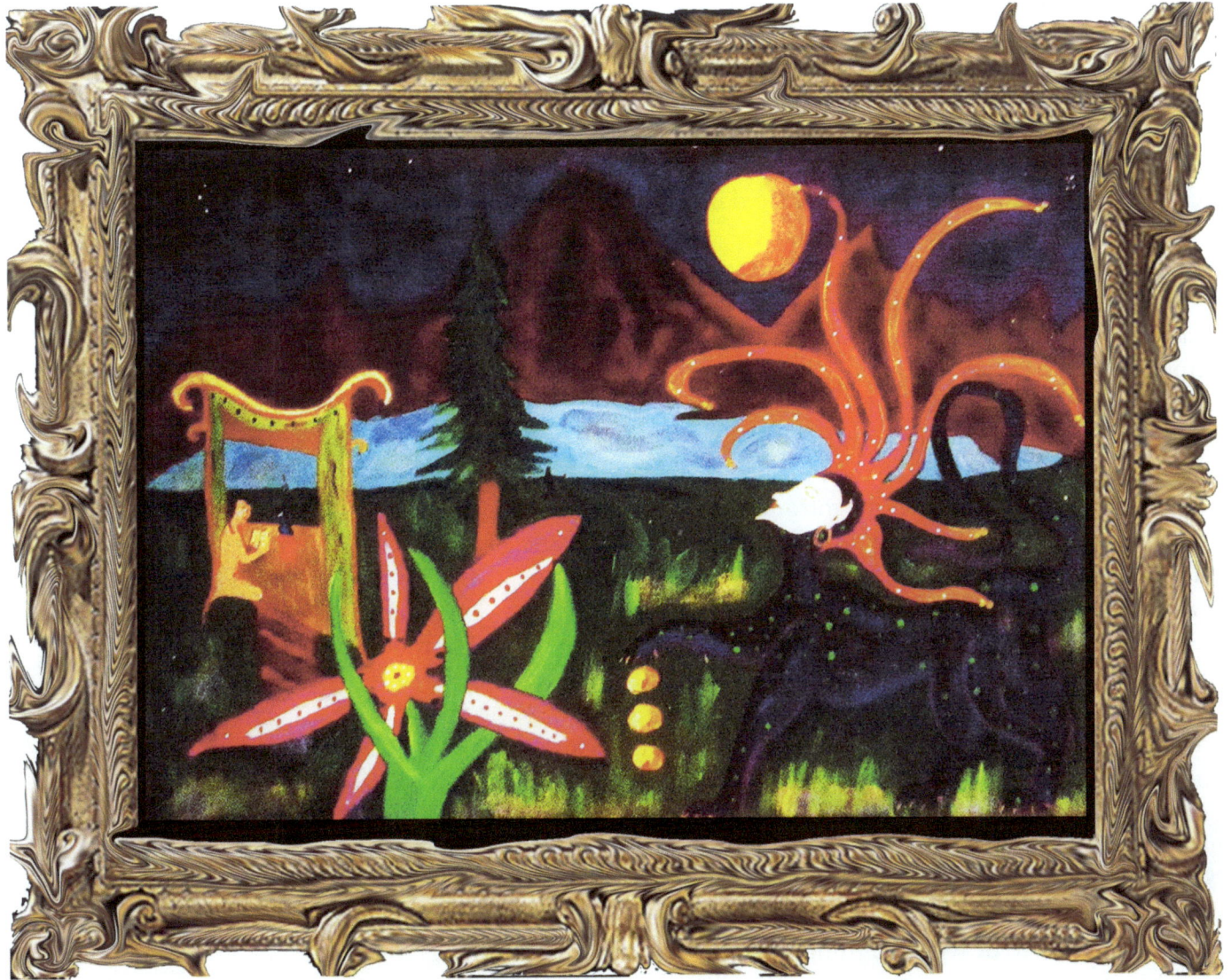

resting. The felina was exuded such compassion, that the glowing mountain behind her responded and at once began to ooze magma. Down long valleys, thin veins of terra firmas blood filled narrow crevices with the energy of a new creative tension. Next to a lone pine by the lake Morgano had appeared as well, and sat waiting for Lolaboy to awaken. In the meantime, the Divine Twin took great pleasure in the serenity of the place.

La Cougera wandered up to the tree and sat next to Morgano. Purring, she said, "Well, here we are. Hmm? What an amazing valley, no? Even magical teachers need sites to recompose and rehabilitate after extensive rites."

"This place… the lake." Morgano took a deep breath. "Is that volcano erupting because of you?"

"Partly so, yes, but I must confess, I sense it is a warning of the drastic changes occurring within the solar galactica forces as well. In some respect, we must just wait now and see… incubate and ponder the emptiness of the wholeness which forms all things. And, as you know, that includes the Dark Mater." La Cougera's coarse tongue stroked her velvety black fur clean. As she did so her lithe body shone even more brilliantly in the morning's glow.

"Do you think Lolaboy is moving or ascending too fast," Morgano inquired? "I mean, of course we'd like to further the evolvolooshun on the planet, but in this Place of Contemplashun, I wonder… if we have *any* power at all during such times. El Universo is constantly recreating itself, the sacred laws upon which we act, the dynamic values we desire to embody, and yet won't you admit, even for the good intention of our mastery, we too must succumb to the deep breaths and exhalations of the grande mystery?"

La Cougera nodded and motioned to Morgano that Lolaboy was stirring in the hut. They watched as heshe sat up and gazed into the fire. Suddenly flames lashed out and flashed in the bungalow. A dark shadow lurched from the fire at Lolaboy. The form shouted, "You desire to control me! I am your unfinished business, the reflekshon of all that has occurred in the corridors of Karmata. You can not hide, nor run from me!"

"Oh dear, come quick Morgano!" Lo Cougera soared through the air like a bolt of lightening in great leaps across the field. Morgano disappeared and then reappeared by the hut.

Lolaboy was frozen in shock. Abrupt and unexpected this enorganica shadow had infiltrated the Place of Contemplashon.

"REVEAL THYSELF! TRUTH CALL OUT YOUR NAME," roared La Cougera! In a flash the fire went cold. What remained were only a few smoldering embers. A few thin plumes of smoke rose into the still air. "Well, *that* was not expected." The moon jaguar turned to Lolaboy. "Weeelll, welcome indeed. I beg your pardon for the rude greeting! Let me introduce myself, I am La Cougera. Morgano is here as well."

"Waaa… waaa… whaaat was that? I was resting peacefully and suddenly felt the urge to wake up, then the fire…," said Lolaboy hysterically.

"We saw everything. Never mind Lola. Take a deep breath." La Cougera placed a paw on Lolaboy's shoulder. Suddenly something grabbed her attention, "Look at that!" The moon jaguar pointed to a flower that had just bloomed next to the hut.

"Perfect timing," said Morgano. "Hello Lotusia."

The flower unfurled its rose petals wide and curled them around the hut. A dense aroma of patchouli and cinnamon permeated the air. "Flora," inquired Lolaboy?

"They are from the same family. This is Lotusia the Flower of Plentifulness." La Cougera softly stroked the plant. "She blooms to remind us, thankfully, about the Language of Light."

"Surely, yes, that's it. The Language of Light! Listen, Lolaboy, if you're going to get any further on this quest… you must be initiated to the synes and simboles of the mythic codes. These will entice the supra-consciousness to be reflected from wherever you are. May I invite us to be silent for a moment. I want you, Lolaboy, to concentrate on the pulses, the vibrations of everything here. For example, can you feel the color of the lake? As it sends out its crystal harmonic chords?"

Lolaboy relaxed alongside their teachers as they helped Lola how to decipher and remember the mystic transmissions of energy. The delicate flow of tones they exhaled from all things. These provided direct access to the amazing tongue of expansiveness, the illustrious symphonic chords that sang the misteries of the universo into being.

"Yes, I… I… do, I can hear everything! How loverly the sounds." Lolaboy gleamed at La Cougera and Morgano. Afterwards, they shared tales of all kinds and warmed their hearts at The Place of Contemplashun. The jaguar magician stayed for a few days and nourished their soulalma.

In a few days Lolaboy was refreshed and rejuvenated. Heshe spent time near the picturesque Lake of Reflekshon and pondered the journey since entering those ominous gates of the Circo de Duendes. Lola had felt very differently since then, thought differently and even moved differently. Morgano and La Cougera shared stories and meals with Lola while also allowing the echoes of deep silence sooth heshe's soulalma. Here, in this wide-open open valley it was possible to dive deep into the sanctuary of the self.

One day, both of heshe's friends approached Lolaboy with inspiration. They invited heshe to sit with them in the beautiful curvy hut. Cougera's paw held a lengthy, carved, mahogany staff. The rod had elaborate colorful images of serpientes coiled around eggs, various planetas and strange calligraphy that was unfamiliar to Lola. Morgano whistled a song into the air:

Tis the rhythm of the night
voyage into the cavernous depths
Transcendent memories float by

Ah, join us night blossoming lotus
Core of the cone
Magic of the crones

Spin this way and that
Weaving the opposites
Spin turn twist and twirl

Tis the momento of refinement
Passing through the alignment
We come to a paradox

Lucent clouds of chance
Dance outside the box
Invoke fresh stories

Into the water that is not wet
Burns fire that does not warm
Unus mundi… We are the Ones!

Spin this way and that
Weaving the opposites
Spin turn twist and twirl

"Well done, dear Morgano, quite the invocation." La Cougera smiled and turned to Lolaboy. "Dear one, a couple other guests will be arriving shortly. I'd like to share a few wisdome procedures with you. For one, you are ready to be taught more about the reasoning behind the *adventurer's quest* you embarked upon so boldly. I feel that you, Lola, are now prepared to assist us with ritual preparations for the sacred wedding of which Luna and Ocelotl had spoken of earlier."

"Yes, please share all you know!" For certain, Lolaboy had wondered from time to time, what this marriage was about, when it would occur, or even how.

"Remember when you had a dream, some time back and the heart and the mind spoke of balancing

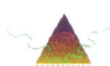

their energies? Lolaboy everything has a rhythm, a definitive vibration and is sequenced to a particular harmony in the cosmos. Certain rhythms, for example, like the beat of your heart, resonate with other intonations filling the atmospheres. The tones relate to each other, harmonizing, creating a vast dynamic melody that conjures the universo itself into being."

La Cougera asked, "Did you ever notice that when you were near a fear gargoyle your heart quickens?" She reached out to touch Lolaboy's chest.

"Yes, it would beat sometimes, very fast. It also does that when I am happy!" exclaimed the jaguar.

"Indeed it does! Well Lola, there are certain rhythms and patterns, which create emphasis for change or lessons to be learned. Once a tone is set, it energizes a blueprint for actions. The Planet of Great Consciousness has layers of these progression designs that enable massive understanding of various principles within the universo." La Cougera looked away towards a wooded area where two red serpientes slithered towards them in the tall lemon green grass.

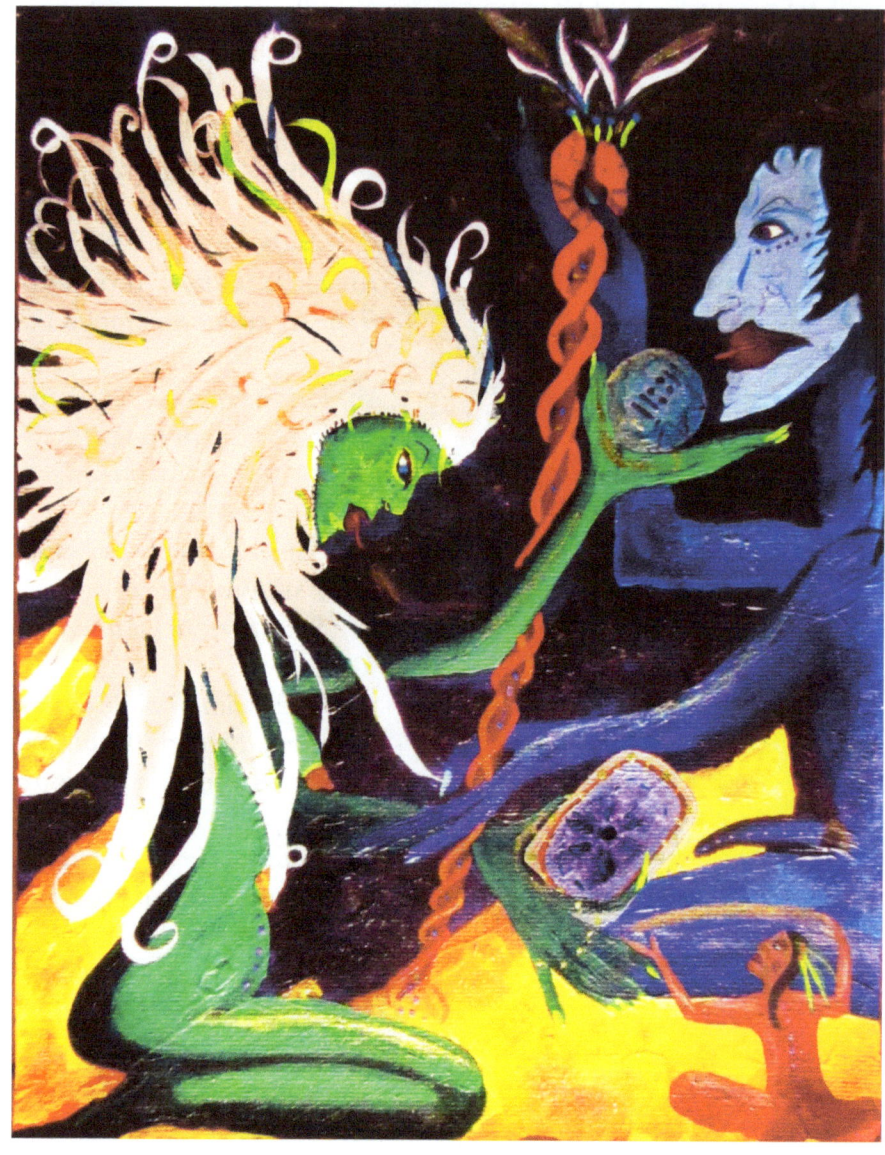

"Our friends have arrived. You may remember one of them Lolaboy, Serpiente Transmuta? He is here with his twin, Vitalia! Welcome to you both, please join our discussion." Morgano moved to one side and the snakes slid onto the wooden floor.

"Sssssooo goood to sssseeee everyone. Lolaboooy, what a loooong time." Transmuta declared. "Morgano, I have transsssported the portal of transsssscendencia, Vitalia will you reveal it pleasssss. Let usssss invite the ground to be abundant."

The serpiente placed a bizarre watery mirror into the circle. While Lolaboy thought it resembled a mirror, its reflection was acting particularly weird.   A haze spiraled in its center; it twisted and swirled, and at times clouds of myst feathered out from the silvery core. On top of that, eerie sounds came from the portal.

Vitalia handed it carefully to La Cougera. The sylphlike puma sat attentively gazing into the mirror for signals that would show the order for the rites. In her other paw was a sphere, which also seemed to mysteriously pulse and quiver with swirling light that rapidly changed colors. Neither of them seemed to perplex La Cougera in the least.

"So good of you to join us dear serpientes… and quickly at that!" La Cougera chimed. "Very well then, let us start the ceremony of activation. Lolaboy, I will explain what we are about to do, and invite you to assist us when I say so."

"I'll do whatever I can", beamed Lolaboy. Heshe was delighted at the invitation to take part in such magic. Up until this point, it seemed that things just happened around heshe; the young jaguar magician yearned to participate more vigorously with the concerns of their friends.

"As I offered earlier, various vibrations contain within them instructions for change and directions on how to navigate through them. A long long time ago, a pulse sparked and was sent throughout the universo affecting the realm of Gaia. A particular sequence was invoked on the blue planeta in order to stimulate growth of the masculine energies. Now it is time to balance those forces because they have spun out of control. Morgano, will you please raise the Staff of Renewal so we can begin our tasks?"

La Cougera explained their course of action further, "Lola, through symbolinas and metaphoras we are able to invoke innovative ideas into action. Hopefully they will be easy to recognize by humanos and thus create prolific response. Hopefully their attention to the sygns will steer them to change outdated and dangerous habits."

La Cougera offered the Portal of Transcendencia to Lolaboy. "Here, take this. After we finish this rite, you may use it to move from one place to another very quickly, with the speed of one thought, you can be anywhere, anytime. Biolocacionata it is called… moving through time and space at will."

"Is this how each of you seem to appear and disappear so quickly," Lolaboy asked?

"Sometimes. Yes," replied La Cougera.

Next to her, Morgano seemed quite occupied. He blew long puffs of air onto the staff while also toning various pleasant-sounding octaves into it. The two serpientes slid into the center of the three and coiled into tight circles. Morgano and La Cougera continued to integrate magical incantations and whispered strange words into the atmosphere surrounding the circle.

"Lolaboy, we are energizing the sacred space and casting a circle of enchantment," Morgano explained.

"One form of magic you may use to summon other jaguar magicians and double-spirits on the planeta, is through the projection. Hence, your own *idea* of self is crucial to how you are representing spirit within the holografica realm. If you harmonize yourself and express consciousness as an integrated, focused beam of amorous light it becomes a beacon of positive magnetism. Hence, Lola, your crystallized thoughts contain attractors… or deflectors… depending on what you focus upon and its intent."

La Cougera continued, "In order to motivate and actualize synchronistic response we're going to invoke crucial aspects of the masculino and femina. These qualities may appear as if they oppose each other however, if we are able to resolve their electrical charges and invite them to polarize instead… there is opportunity for… well… the wedding of force. After, the opposition dissolves and the differences between the masculino and feminina properties unify again and become one… separation ends. The planeta can ascend into a new dimensione.

Unfortunately, those that express tendencies to unify the different genderas, such as the jaguar magicians, are often cursed and tortured on the blue planeta. The tormentors have used ill will upon those that engage this type of balancing of the genderas inside themselves. When they harm them they damage the spectrum of likelihood on the planeta. Hence, it has been a terrible and arduous struggle for many years based upon misrepresented rationale from single preferencia relgionas, and draconia goviernos.

Alas, there is a discouraging deceptive delusion and perilous desire for control of the planeta. Much of this has an underlying tone with regards to one form of sexualidad dominating the other and, then of course, their inherent principles being censored." La Cougera raised her left paw and swirled the radiating sphere around the staff in Morgano's right hand.

"What is that globular thing? It keeps changing colors," asked Lolaboy?

"This is a polarization orb. It is used to anchor specific tones to the rod." La Cougera focused on the staff and began to chant:

Twelve twelve to the thirteen twenty
Twelve twelve into the thirteen twenty
Twelve twelve to blend with the thirteen twenty

Combing the contraries
Summon the faeries
Raise the ferraimune's staff
Twelve Twelve to the thirteen twenty

Union of energies
Everything as one
Logic and intuition
Process and goal

Blossom oh golden rod
Clockwise and counter
Down into the ground
Twenty times the thirteen

Universal consciousness
Rise from the irony
Of separation from the celestial
Reconfigure the governance
Bring peace between them

La Cougera motioned to Serpiente Transmuta and Vitalia to move closer,

Rise up from the realm of limitless possibilities
Aspects of Vitalia
Facets of Transmuta

Become ONE!
Join to turn into a single form
The Caduceusious is now born!

The two snakes glided effortlessly up the pole and intertwined into a spiral oneness. Morgano raised the staff to the sky. La Cougera spun the spheric orb around the staff. Lolaboy watched and at once felt a vibration spark from the Portal of Transcendence. The misty plumes reached higher and higher into the air and enveloped the staff.

Unus Mundi!
Connected as One!

La Cougera, Morgano and the rod began to fade into the mysts from the Portal of Transcendencia. Lolaboy gaped at the spectacular images before them. Golden crystals formed, an arco iris spanned a purple horizon, dazzling blue stars splashed across the sky, and the portal reflected hundreds of images within seconds. Each picture faded quickly until one of them held firm. Lolaboy saw Ocelotl in the portal.

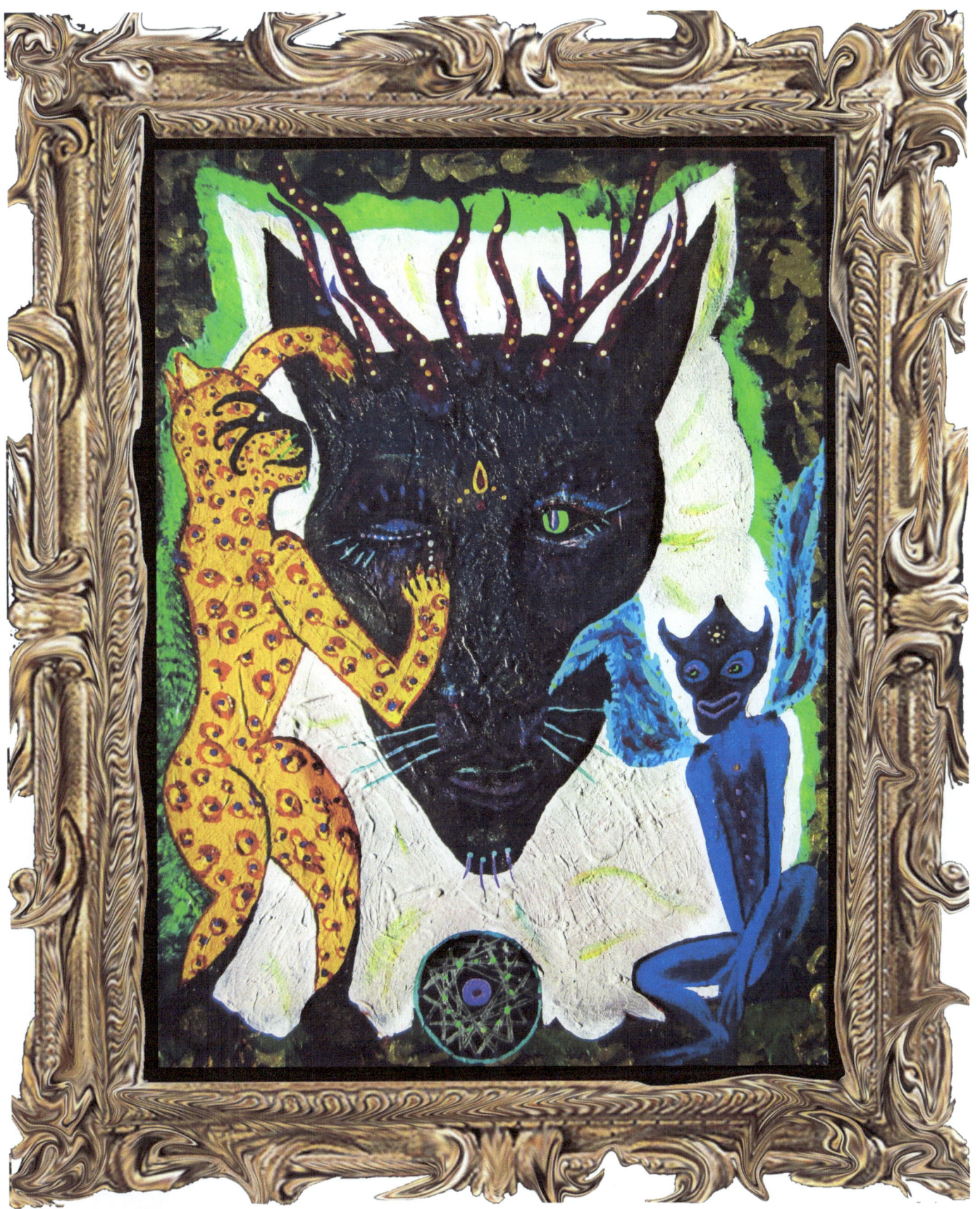

$\mathcal{B}$efore Lolaboy could even contemplat Ocelotl further, heshe was there! Lola stood next to the master surrounded by a thick forest of curling ferns and all manner of astonishing flowers. There were strange new whistles and chirps of birds. This woodland was like no other Lola had been on his journey. There was also a cacophony of buzzing of insects and sounds that resembled hysterical laughter. The noise boomed from the mossy verdant thickness of craggy branches.

Standing next to Ocelotl was an enormous white lion with twisted horns and a striking mahogany face full of wooly white fur with bluish feathers. Flying around the trees was an electric blue creatura. It giggled and darted here and there in the canopy. Then it dove and flew directly towards Lolaboy, while taunting them a bit.

"*Who*… whoo are you?" Lolaboy reached into the air for the unusual being. "Ocelotl, where am I?" Heshe turned toward the master jaguar. The young magician felt somewhat dizzy and plopped onto the ground.

The jaguar maestro did not reply; it seemed as though Ocelotl could not hear or even see Lolaboy. The blue creatura landed on the tip of a frond spiking from within a cluster of ferns. It grinned at the young jaguar magician.

"I am the blueberrie faerie! I've been called in by Auntie Oshedante. Uh, and just so you know, your *friend*, Ocelotl is behind the *veil*." The whimsical creatura flapped delicate, transparent wings and flew off into the air above Lolaboy.

> *Tit for tat*
> *Did you think I was a bat?*
> *Yantra see*
> *Mantra glee*
> *Teardrop raindrop*
> *Into the lake I plop*
>
> *For giving*
> *To the living*
> *Light of a thousand suns*
> *Time for a revolushun!*
> *River glow*
> *However slow*
> *Sent by Auntie Oshedante*
> *And there is nothing to rhyme with that!*

The blueberry faerie raced off into the treetops. Lolaboy observed Ocelotl move closer to the grande snowy felina. It looked like the cat was weeping. Large silver tears fell from its right eye. Ocelotl raised his paw and gathered them. One by one as they fell slowly from the creaturas deep-set eye.

Ocelotl reverently addressed everyone. "Dear Whitelionmeetswhitebuffalowomon, I now hold the silver tears. They contain in them the power of complete forgiveness. Through this conduit of mercy comes complete happiness. Thank you for this gift." The jaguar teacher turned to where Lolaboy sat. "Rise, Rise, into the eternal, all points within the universo, I deliver the message of love and amnesty to all beings… sovereignty to all!" The great jaguar waved his hand and tossed the tears into the air… dispersing them into the atmosphere. The ground violently shook and an enormous black hole appeared where they had stood. Then, there was nothing but stillness; there was only deep silence where nothingness permeated.

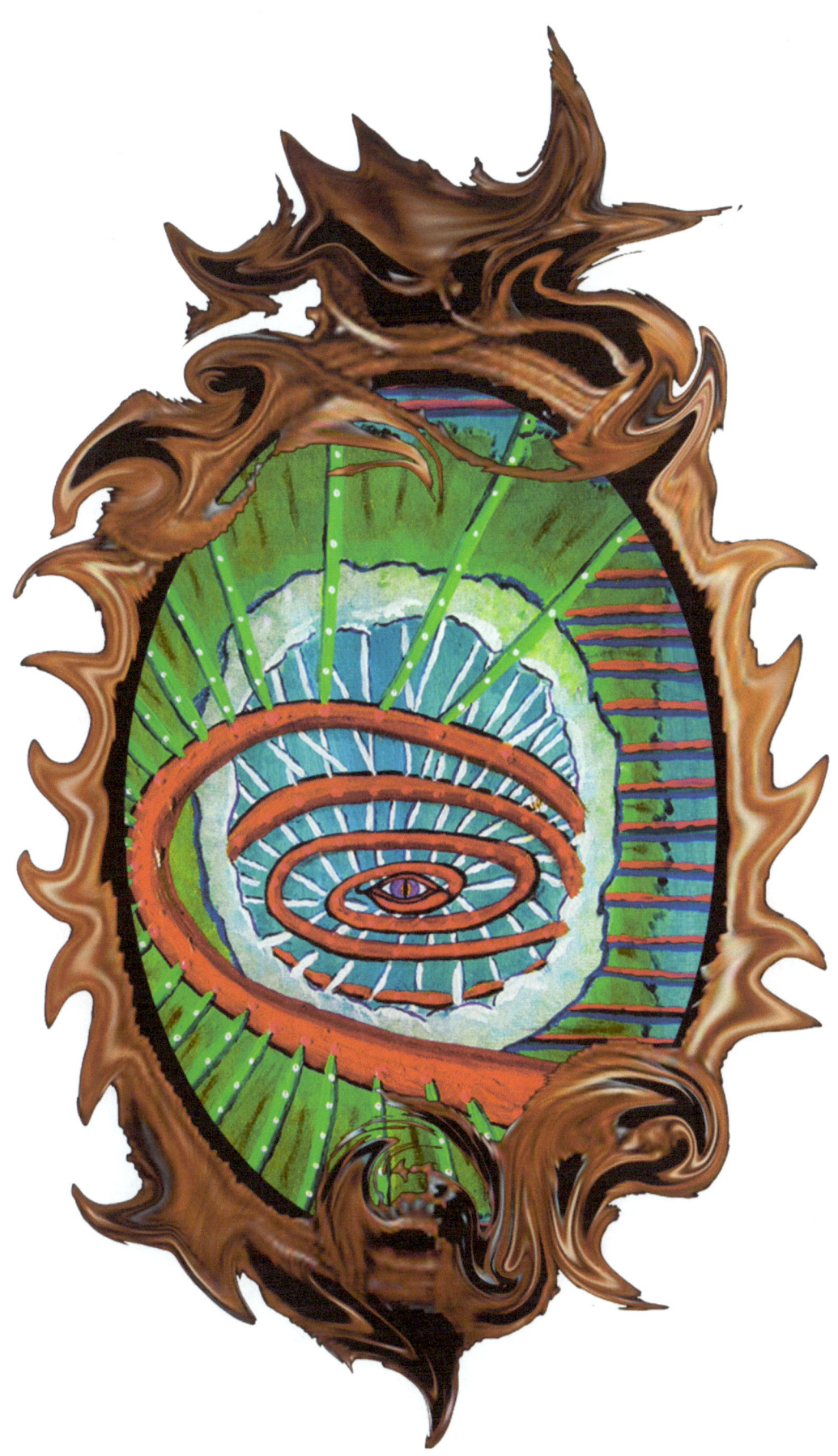

From the darkness rose a dull amber glow. It pulsed and sputtered and then it blazed bright red and laser lemon yellow. The bold colors swirled and formed a whirlpool of electrical charged fiery mass. It spun so fast it turned to a pure white light, like a solar quasar, dazzling to the eye. Lolaboy shielded their eyes.

A voice boomed from the ray of light. "I am the light of a thousand suns. I am that I am. I come from the place of all thoughts. I am the all-knowing observer. I have received the message of care and absolution. I hereby open the path to the Aguila Grid. At this juncture is the entrada. Awakened is the Flora de Vida. I shine upon the way to the core of governing matrices for the Planet of Great Consciousness and all other formed frequency arcs that affect the realm of Gaia."

Lolaboy watched in awe as a vivid eye formed at the center of a bellowing, flashing, blindingly white cloud. From the center of the opening curved a large red ribbon like a trail. It spiraled out and out, reaching towards Lola. Just then, great jade steps appeared. Each of them was adorned with small golden points of light.

"I am the place of the eternal now, the dimension where all separations point to zero. This is the nucleus of existence. Step into the place of centeredness; it is here one realizes the laws of sacred geometry. In this core it is possible to participate and acquire the skill of discernment. Here one may witness the vast library, which holds all language. The annals stored here encompass the entire continuum of memory and probability."

All at once, as if pulled upon or hypnotized, Lolaboy dreamily stood up and staggered onto the fiery red thoroughfare, into the depths of the unknown known.

Suspended in the air around Lolaboy hung numerous objects. Floating in midair were several double reversed pyramids and octahedronicos. There were also hundreds of bizarre arrays of lines and spheres. Everything twirled in space illumined with tangerine light.

Who am I? Lolaboy considered using the question again. However heshe felt by now this question was somewhat redundant. Instead, heshe remembered what Pumana Peakok had offered, *a magician knows how to ask the right questions.* Lolaboy pondered this, and asked another, "Why am I here and what did I just pass through?"

Several of the forms acted, and magnetized to each other. They fashioned themselves into what looked like letters. However if it was such an attempt, it was an alphabet unknown to Lolaboy. While in La Selva, the young magician had been taught to read and write many languages, however this one made no sense at all. It was completely alien.

"Pssst… Lola, it's me, Morgano. You are in the Annals of the Epoch. Chambers in this library contain all the glyphs, sacrado geomancy, symbolinas of all time and no time." Morgano rushed up from below to where Lolaboy was suspended in mid-air. The jaguar magician revolved within a large gelatinous sphere.

"What am I to discover here? I do not understand any of these images. Can you help me?"

An oversized balloon, or it could have been a vase, formed below Lolaboy. Protruding from the tip of its neck were two plush red lips. "Spiral, concept, tetrahedronakal, faces of the grid. Welcome to the archetypal codifiers that form the doorway to greater conscious awareness. I am Creestolatl the Grid Geomanizer. You know my cousin, Ametist Mal O Kyte Rutilated Quartzessa, the Gatekeeper."

The bulbous lips pursed and out burst several incredible geometric shapes. They continued to bubble forth one after another. Heshe had never seen such exquisite shapes.

"These are symbolical metaforia for life. How it forms and attaches to ideas, possibilities, and tendencies."

Inside some of the shapes, were tiny balls of white light. "What are *those*?" asked Lolaboy.

"In the order of the galactical WOW, these introduce the particulata of the divino aminatas and engage, what you call unbound spirit or ideas. Thereby, they increase their ability to relate one thing to another,

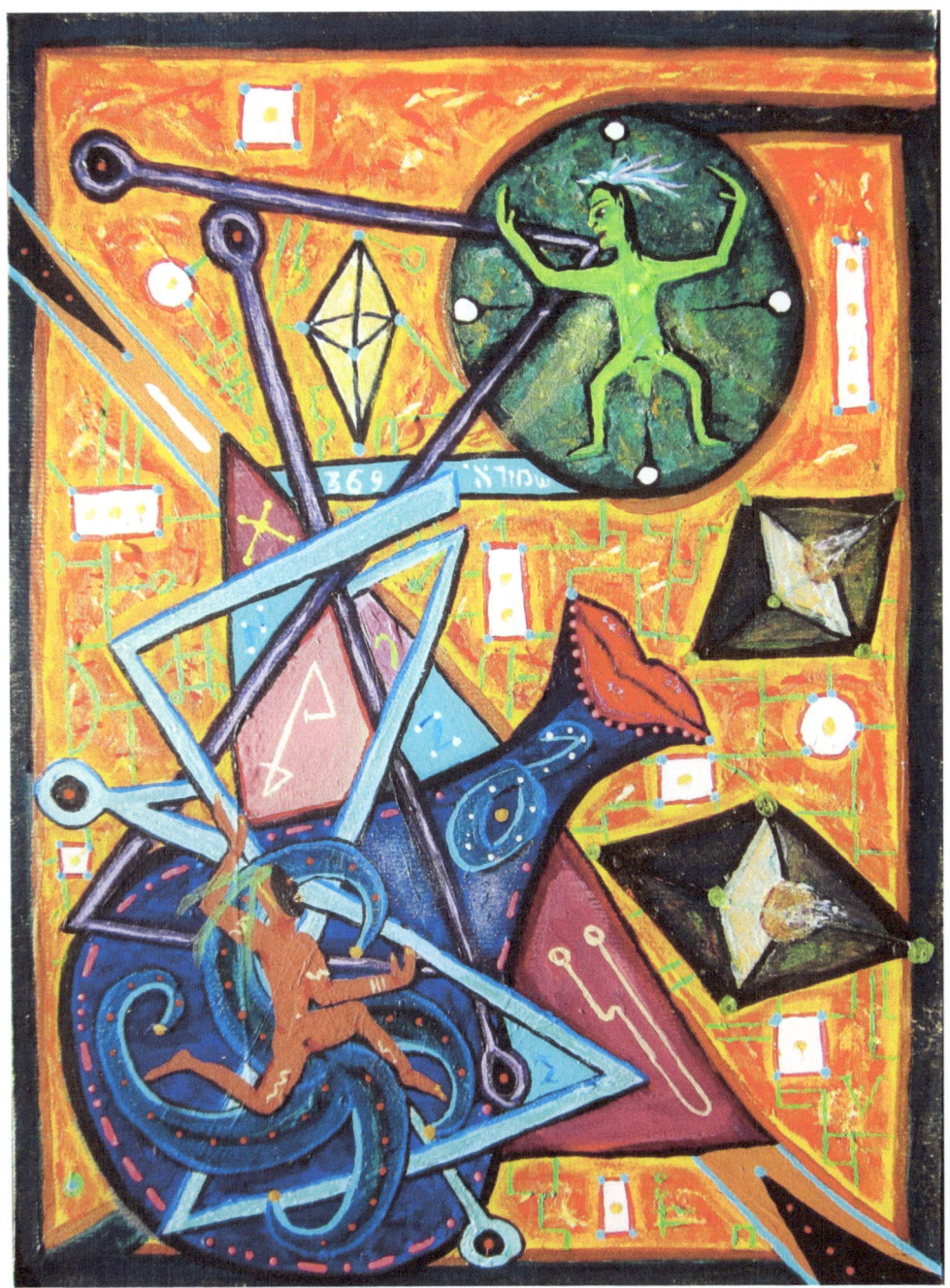

like organization or symbiositicota." The crimson mouth wafted out more forms from its protruding ruby orifice. Several lines shaped themselves into a network. "These are the Illumination Lattices."

Lolaboy watched as an electric bolt of piercing white light rushed along the lines. As it went on its way, squares, rectangles and a few circles formed. "Honestly? I am completely confused." The young jaguar watched as the grid sprawled and spawned more and more of its vast network until the entire area was covered with a lattice.

"ME TOO," chortled Creestolatl! "I'm a-fused too! Hahahahah! Jaggy, it's about *concepts*. From the complexa to the simplica, to the unusual, to the redundant. Once the complexata shifts, there's no turning back tho," harped the Geomanizer.

"Lolaboy, it's not important for you to understand everything in its entirety. This is to stimulate your memory field with the vast language of order. The foundation of everything depends on how patterns form and reform, how they relate and evolve into something completely new or different. This is the state of affairs within the realm of Gaia. The planeta is being introduced with new codigos and thereby presented with a greater tendency to master the dualidad and separation of opposites." Morgano continued to hover in front of the sphere while Lolaboy twirled in space.

"When you arrive back on the planeta again one day, you will see that there is abundant technologia which has perilously reversed sacred rhythm into a state of destructive chaotica," stated Morgano. "For now, just consider that numbers and patterns are more *significant* than many of the humanos comprehend. However, the fresh tones of the jaguar magicians, the one's we hope that you will mirror for them may perhaps reflect that energy cohesively and empathically. These will awaken them to a greater understanding… like yours. Hopefully it will eventually engage the collective realization how to actively rebuild and catalyze a new matrix around Gaia. It will bring about a more harmonic path for everyone and everything there *and* in the entire universo."

Lolaboy sensed that the sphere was falling. It plummeted with heshe, diving deep into space. Morgano disappeared, as did the Geomanizer. Once again Lolaboy was left in a still place, although this one was filled with abundant white light.

*S*pinning and falling deep into the unknown like water down a drain Lolaboy fell to *somewhere*… again. Heshe was a bit exhausted with this frantic pace. Alas, I would never know as much as Morgano, Lola thought. How was I supposed to wake up the other two-spirits? I'd never even met one! Lolaboy continued to levitate in the empty space.

"You're soooo right… you'll *never* catch up to 'em Lolaboy. Why bother? It's not your mess. Return to La Selva, or come with us", hissed a voiced in the emptiness. "You know… it's not as bad as they say on the planeta. Plenty of humanos are completely happy and enjoying the chaotica. Who do you think you are anyway Lolaboy? Or, your supposed '*friends*' for that matter!"

"Honestly, I don't know any longer what *most* of this is about! I took this *adventurer's quest*, walked through mirror after mirror and gate after gate. And I still don't know why I am here, or really what I am to do? Why do these other walks-betweens even need me? Can't they do this on their *own*? I don't know half of what Ocelotl knows, why can't he go there? Or Gaia, can't she help them? Aren't there other places for the humanos to go, through the portals, to live, if they want?" Lolaboy violently shook their fist into the air thrusting heshe's arm so hard that the jaguar nearly fell over.

"Look here little jaguar, come with us! We're your friends. We *understand* the part of you that feels unworthy, untrusting. If you join us, we shall teach you how to feed on their problemas and get strong, and if you want, the potential to control consciousness…"

Something stirred in the white light and moved swiftly, raising chills on Lolaboy's spine. Heshe's energy abruptly quivered and dizziness set in, Lolaboy fainted.

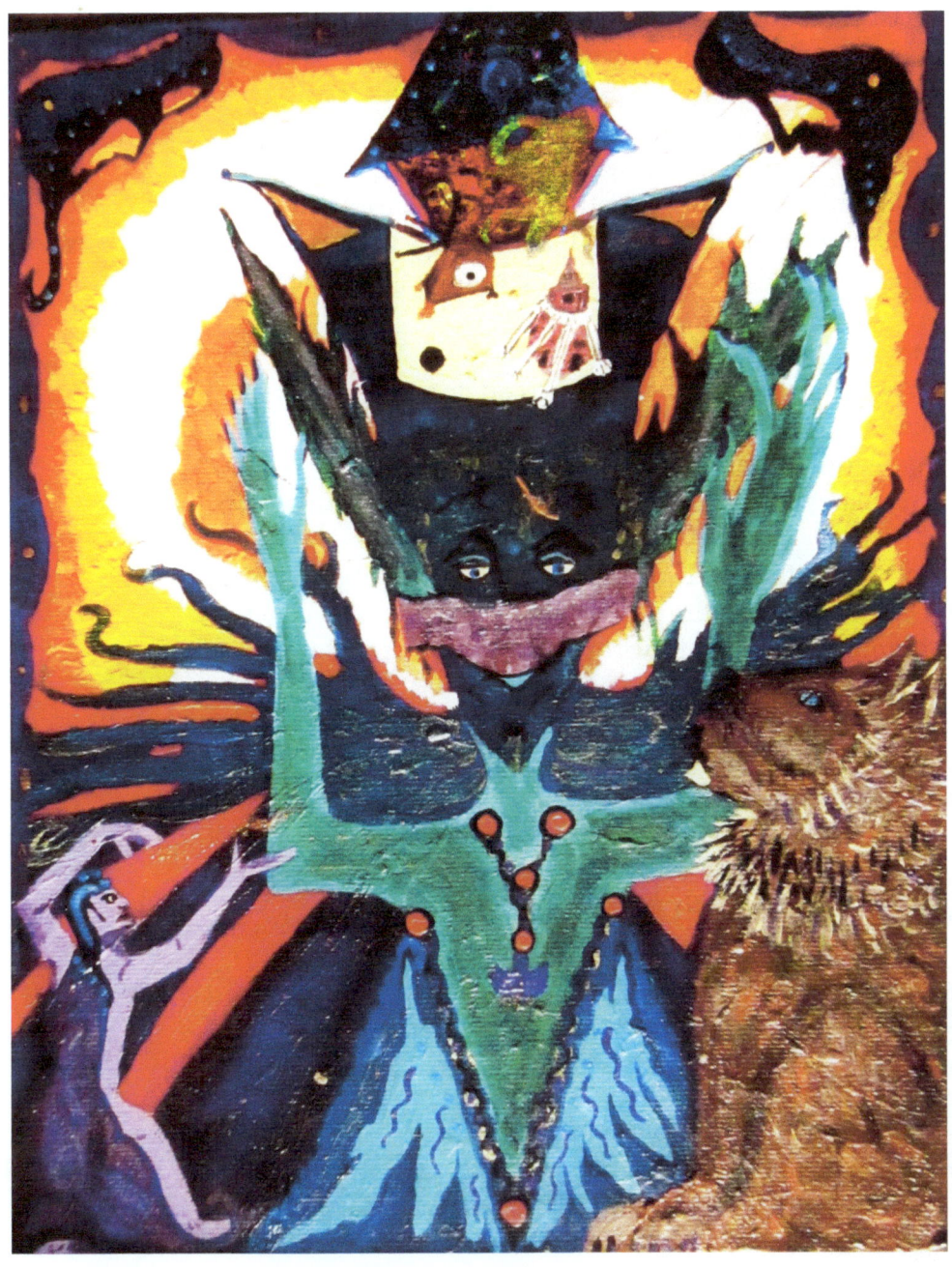

Zing zang zap
With a snap
Be gone irractic enorganics
Ping pang pop
You shall flop
Disengage sporadic entities
Ding Dang Dop!
No more of this slop
Off into the nethers
Sing sang sap
Tether not to this flap
Wither nither triggernauts
Hing hang hop
This jaguar is NOT
What you thought!

"Now be gone!" ordered Ocelotl. The master jaguar raised his paw and with a whoosh… the Enorganics were disposed of and dispersed. He bent over Lolaboy and dropped some of the silver tears of forgiveness onto heshe's crown. "Now… Lolaboy return to this quest. You *have* the strength and willingness. Here! Here! Collapse the contrary self!"

Lolaboy began to stir, slowly blinking their eyes until they focused on the jaguar maestro. At first, Lola wasn't sure they could trust the image before their eyes. It could have been Ocelotl, or it could be something else — a mirage.

"Dear dear, you *did* have a shock. It is I. *Trust.*" Ocelotl waved his paw over Lola's chest. "Look here, I'll show you a trick, some magia if you will, and then you shall see that it also lives within thee!"

Lolaboy sighed, "Alright, I see you. I know it's you." Heshe turned and saw a huge being had appeared. "What is that?!"

"A double-spirit. Or rather a *prototype* for a double-spirit, a sort of effigy we can practice upon… with a willingness to transform." Ocelotl put out his paw and Lolaboy tightly clutched it. Together they approached the monstrous figure. "No need to fear anything here. Now observe for a moment. Tell me what you see. Do you sense anything unusual?"

The huge form had a beautiful emerald teal gown from which hung iridescent aqua feathers. It was adorned with elegant red gems. What was most interesting, was that the being, or double-spirit model, had a cloth tied around it's head which covered its mouth.

"I sense a struggle. I see a handsome being. I feel that there is something feeding it... or forcing it to do something?" Lolaboy observed as a ghastly orifice opened atop its head. Several items began to fall from the sky into the gaping hole on its head. It looked like a box with a glass screen, a building with pillars, and a gold statue of a masculine figure. They all seemed to pour into the space that filled the head of the being.

"Well done. Here are things that stand for ideas which govern a current two-spirit's paradigmia. Religioso, governada, and the tekno realms attempt to fool or entrap a double-spirit's consciousness, sabatoging its will to live. Together we'll initiate and stimulate patterns in order to weave a template for new consciousness." Ocelotl turned to Lolaboy and motioned to heshe. "I'll stand on one side with you on the other."

"But why is that cloth around its mouth," wondered Lolaboy?

"Ah... it's a piece of fabric that represents ignorancia that spawned on its own to cover the voice of truth as a result of the malicious influences that flood its mind. These external systems of thought, that do not comply with the greater good, have forced themselves upon the innocencia of a double-spirit and other humanos. It's formed a trap. This snares their ability to perceive things and changes their ability to instinctually respond."

"That hole above its head, is that one of the rips that I've heard of... in the netting of consciousness?" Lolaboy pointed to the immense gape in the sky above the effigy.

"Yes. Now, we shall cast a spell to restore the universal laws of integrity so that these systems become transparent and the truth is revealed. A pock ov Lipstow!"

Ocelotl thrust his velvety mitts into the air and aimed them at the effigy. "Now do as I and repeat with me... imagine that from the tips of our fingers flow beams of laser blue light. We can invite in change... focus your intention onto the snare of cloth."

> *Hiddidididy ho!*
> *Heydididy ho!*
> *Addicted to strife*
> *Mentiriactical conundrums*
> *Religioso, governada, tekno*
> *No more full of delusia*
> *Self aware you become*
> *Hiddidididy ho!*
> *Heydididy ho!*
> *Awaken double-spirit*
> *Model of all*
> *Weaving the fabric of collectiva*
> *We insert the laws of integrity*
> *Hiddidididy ho!*
> *Heydididy ho!*

With all heshe's might, Lolaboy focused every thought onto the being that stood paralyzed before them. The youthful magician repeated the chant three times with Ocelotl. Soon after, there was a stirring, then a great wind surged and swirled around the double-spirit effigy. "NO MORE," cried out Lolaboy!

All at once, the cloth hiding the beings' mouth shredded itself and the pieces blew away in the storm. Astonished by the affect of their combined will, Lolaboy smiled and ran to Ocelotl and hugged him.

"There... now, why would you *doubt* yourself? Hmm? I want you to practice some of the magia you have learned on your way… prepare yourself… for soon, you will work with the Lunas, Gaia and others on continuous reweaving of patterns for the planeta. Now I shall send Transmuta to guide you with a technique on how to perform metamorphosis upon the opposing fractal of polarities. This field is very strong around the planeta now." Ocelotl patted Lolaboy on the back. "Well done, jaguar! Well done!"

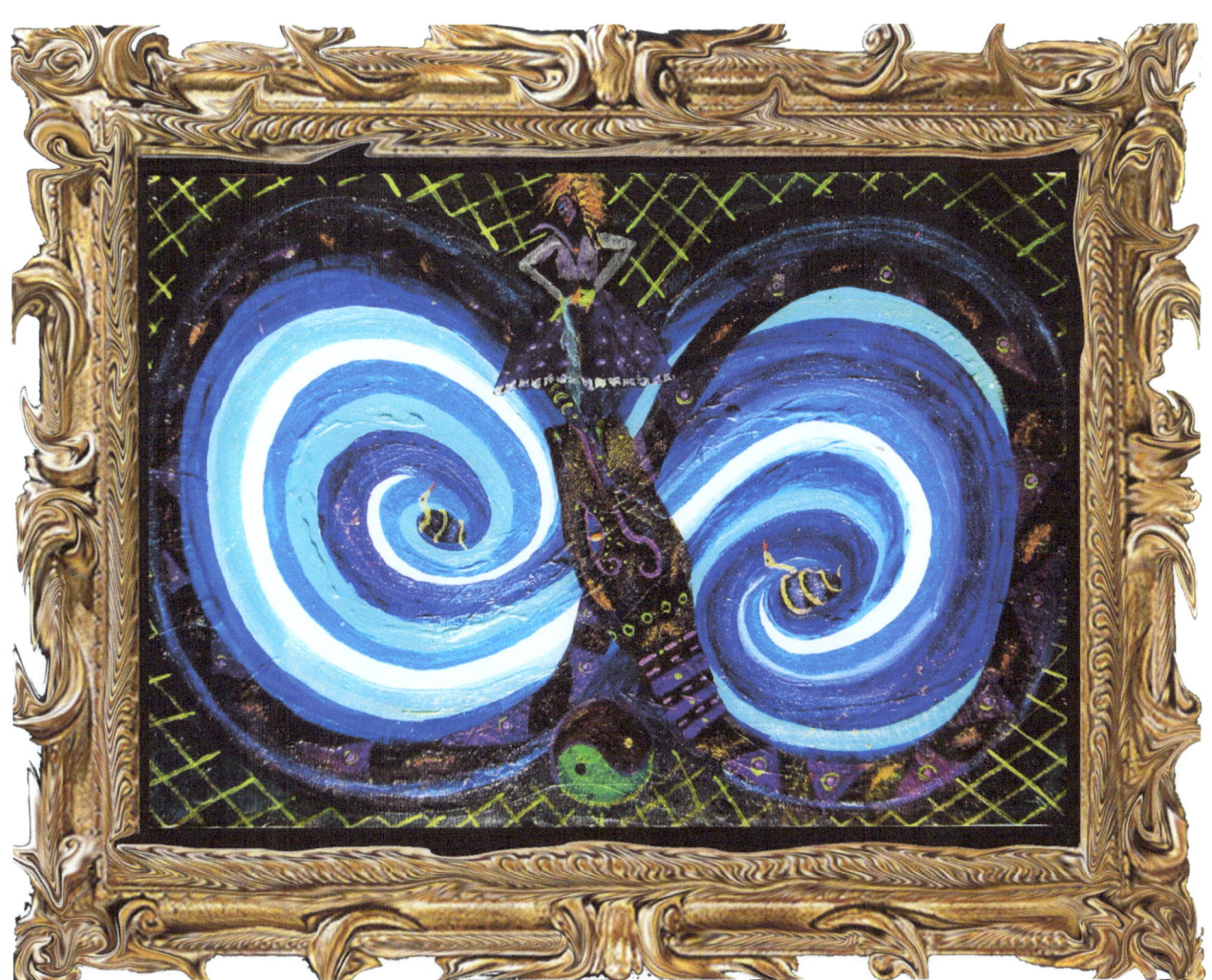

*O*celotl disappeared into a thicket of fertile forest, while Lolaboy waited for Transmuta the Serpiente to appear. Lola reflected on what had just occurred. How fantastic to see magia in action! More than ever, something had stirred and awakened deep within Lolaboy, a feeling never felt before. Heshe had observed the power of thought.   Focused intent could affect an event inevitably so that it changed reality... for the greater good. Moment by moment the strife from doubt and apathy left the young jaguar's heart.

Darting back and forth, zigzagging across the moss covered forest floor, Transmuta slithered next to Lolaboy. The serpiente then formed itself into the twisted shape of a figure eight.

"Thisssss issssss the codigo for rezzzzolusssshun of dualidad. Eezzzeee. Now you do it," slurred the snake.

"I can't do that!" giggled Lolaboy. "You are amazing, Transmuta!"

"Mirrored back at you," hissed the snake. "Ah… well, yessss then, perhapsssss, you can't do *egggsssactly* thissss with your body, but you do have a ssssspine and it curlsssss ssssomewhat asssss well…"

The snake unraveled itself and coiled up on the ground next to Lolaboy. With its tail it flapped 2 golden eggs back and forth in the air. Each of them had tiny serpientes wound about them.

"Awesome, how did you do that? And...what are those?" Lolaboy pointed to the eggs.

"Ah, they represssent, metaforica, for power of potenseeaa. Alssso, the capabiliteessss. Now, watch thissss!" Transmuta, amusing himself, again fashioned his body into a figure eight with the two eggs at the center of the circular forms. "Now let'sss do ssssome amalgamation of possssssibilitiesss. Do you sssstill have the Krysssstal of Clarity or the talc of Dusssty Miller?"

"Why, I *do*!" Lolaboy pulled them out of deep pockets in the purple robes. "*And*, I have the key, that the Keeper of the Masques gifted me."

"Perfect! Now, think of a chalasssse, an elegant one, sssssuitable for an elixxxir." The serpiente levitated in front of Lolaboy.

"Ok. I have the chalice in mind."

"Now, put the cryssssstal and ssssome of the talc into the cup. Ssstir it with the key. We are going to focusss our intention on dissssssolving the illussssion of two, thisss and thaaaat... dualidad."

A mammoth web fell down from the forest canopy. Drums rattled from somewhere within each of the tree trunks. A bird sang and whistled an inspiring, soothing lullaby. Cricketas chirped.

Orbica shells holding potencia
Polarity rupture schism
We call you forth
To affect the whole
Upon the 8 of the 8
Infinite change
Ribbons of consciousness
Vow to cleanse
The illusory film
Upon this time and place
Upon the 8 of the 8
We place upon the slate
To open the gate
And release the hate
The noose of fear
Duality, complementary, opposing
Behaviors bewitched and belittled
Changing points of reference
We lay the lines into this plane
Solutions resolutions!
Upon the 8 of the 8
Snate snate snake!

"It issss done! It issss done! It issss done! Hooray!" Transmuta hissed and untied himself, then went and wrapped his thin, cordlike body around a tree. "There, you've jussssst had a coursssse in Magica 101. Now I mussssst resssst, my dear... between assssisting my family Vitalia and the otherssss from the rod healing *and* thissss, all good creaturass need to pausss once in a while. Reflect. Retreat... retreat...retreat..." Serpiente slithered into a hole in the dirt next to the curling roots of a cyprusitica tree.

Lolaboy was tired as well and lay down on the ground to dream once again in the forest. It was one of heshe's favorite activities.

*I*n this dream, Lolaboy was with Morgano, in a large bubble. Someone was holding a globular form in the air, laughing hysterically.

"Wahahaha. Woohooo. Payaso Pineyal for sure, I am!" The round faced man chuckled. The clown's head was too large for his body and he had three eyes. Only one of them was open at the center of his forehead.

M A O
Whoa!
Inhibit snibbit.

Pine Cone
Opening

Weeeeeee

Veil of reality
Cloak of mystery
Core submission

M A O, NO!
Ho! Ho! Ho!

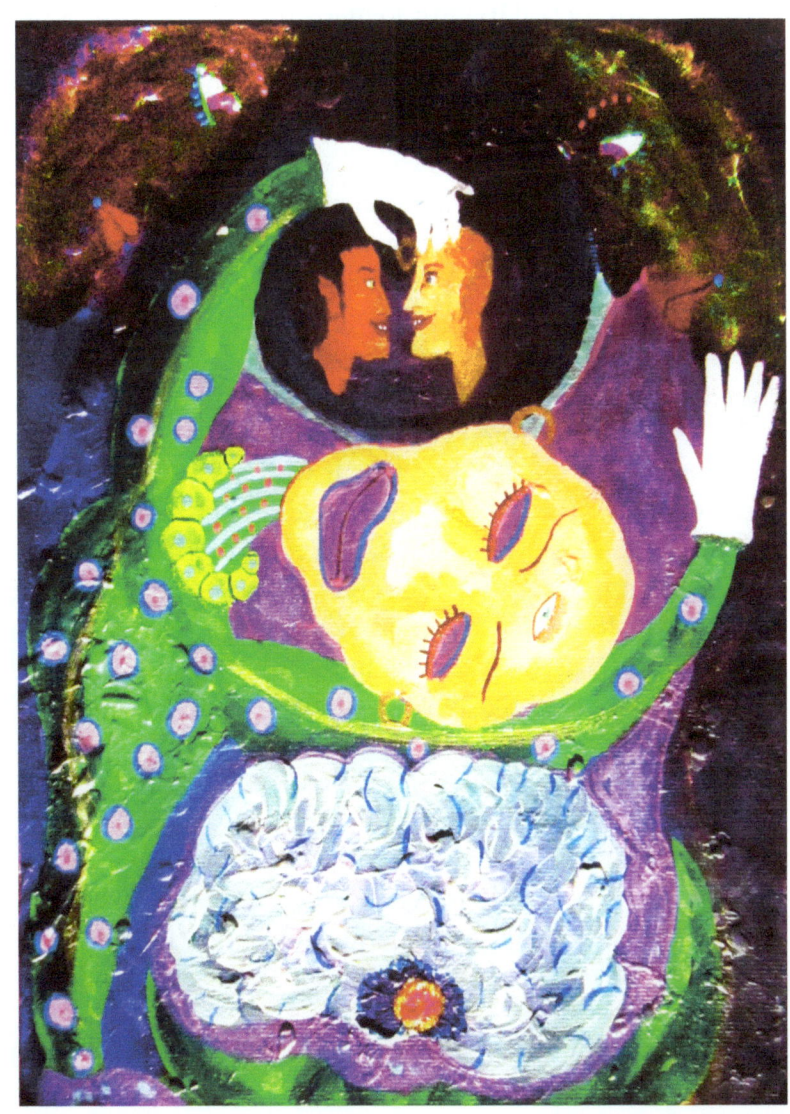

"Well, well, well. Look at you two… romancing the stone. Bahahahaha," chortled the payaso! "Which one of you is right brain or left brain? Or are you one of the NO brains? Weeeeehehehehehehee!" The payaso danced in a circles and bounced the bubble with Morgano and Lolaboy inside it.

"Eh, payaso, stop rolling us around!" yelled Morgano with a grin.

"Roll, roll, roll your brain gently down the lane. Like no other you shall be if you awaken thee!" Payaso Pineyal bent over and turned upside down. The top of his head opened and out plopped a spongy brain.

"Say heeeeelooo to Sara Bellyum! Ain't she a bute?" Payaso's voice boomed and echoed, which vibrated the surface of the bubble.

The globbulous globe oozed and emitted an iridescent opalescent liquid.

"Tastes just like chi-ken. Bah. Snooze you dooze. Soak in this jism and then the walls fall. You can see it all!" Payaso picked up the Sara Bellyum and squeezed it over the bubble onto Lolaboy and Morgano.

"Yup, build this bridge. Unify the selves. Liberate the slaves! Divine twins regenerate they have. Boy, am *I* glad." The clown grinned at them. His smile was so that big the edge of their lips protruded from the sides of his face.

"Can't open unless you unleash the clown! Bahahahahhahaah!"

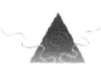

_Lolaboy woke up, or so they thought, maybe it actually was still a dream? Who knows? Heshe remained with Morgano. A choir hummed a haunting melody in the distance. Above them was el Sol and la Luna, however it was a Luna that Lolaboy had never seen. This one was purple. Morgano sat smiling directly across from Lolaboy. In between them was a beautiful sphere with sapphire, aqua, and indigo swirls. Small lime green manzana fruits began to slowly fall from the sky. Lolaboy caught one and held it up to Morgano.

"How wonderful to have so many manzanas! How strange they're so many falling from the sky. Where are we now, Morgano?" Lolaboy gathered more of the fruits and piled them between their legs.

"Taste one… see what happens. They're not just any fruit." Morgano took one of the symmetrical fruits and bit into it. As he did so, the blue sphere between them began to pulse. A vine or perhaps a tree, began to sprout, and grow, grow, grow from its core. Within moments, there stood a large heart shaped tree waving in the air high above the two magicians.

"A good sign," said Morgano. "It shows we have roots in many directions, throughout multi-dimensions of space." The Divine Twin peered up at the towering tree and grinned wider as the celestial beings Sol and Luna came closer to them.

"Ah… look here, the twins have arrived! I am Sun Runner of the Tribal Sol and my partner, Muluca of Luneria, the Moon Seer. Would you like to play a game with us," asked the brilliant yellow sun?

"Of course," gleamed Lolaboy!

Sun Runner reached into the air with his hand. He adjusted a triangular frame. Muluca did the same from her side. They twirled them together in the air and spun them around the unusual tree.

"See if you can get one of the fruits through the triangles while we keep moving them up and down. This is a game to help you focus on your center." The sun and the moon laughed as they rotated, lifted and swerved the triangular forms.

Morgano tossed a manzana into the air toward one of the forms in Sun Runner's hand. It slipped easily through the hole. After that the silhouetted pyramid froze in its place next to one of the curved limbs of the tree.

"Wow, that was cool! Let me see if I can do it." Lolaboy raised their arm, pitched the fruit… _Bullz-eye_," laughed the jaguar magician!

Two triangular shapes were now frozen in place. Sun Runner and Muluca pulled out two more identical forms. Morgano and Lolaboy aimed manzanas at them; each hit their target freezing the frames in place. The new triangles were filled with golden turquoise powder.

"Now, try to get a fruit through the two of them at the same time." Sun Runner winked at Muluca. "Focus… Ready. Set. Go!"

Together, the two magicians aimed and cast the fruits toward the forms. Again they went through with ease, and perfectly into the center. With that, the heart shaped tree blossomed at once with two more hearts, one black and one gold.

"What is this game," Lolaboy inquired?

"It's a pastime known as Kryonus. It hones the skill of awakened attention and if you aimed well, as both of you did, it raises octaves of the trinity matrix to form a twelfth dimensional shield. This shield is used like a dimensional portal. You can concentrate and move onto other points of light."

Lolaboy looked at Morgano while scrunching their brow.

"Ah, ha! Haha. Sun Runner, you speak in tongues that confuse my twin. Lola, remember I sent you to visit Grandmother Spider? Zuvuyana shared the story of the trinities? Now, if you take two trinities, they of course make six points. The more options one considers, the greater the possibility of something coming into expression or form."

Muluca had been silent through most of the game and felt a stirring to speak. "Ah ha! My precious jaguars… Lolaboy, in the library with the Geomanizer, you learned of frequencies, and harmonies. These fruits are nourishing your wisdom, that also helped with your ability to find a center equilibrium when there's disruption in the frequency waves around you. So, if you hear shadow temptations or seductions, you can form a shape, such as this triangle, and focus your will, your intent and send it through. And, voi la! You are on the other side and in the realm of the desired outcome. This is also referred to as a zero pointifica combination."

The moon continued, " Lolaboy, once you are on the planeta again, you will have a dynamic vibration quite different from the others. However, you can and shall mirror this harmony onto all things that you come into contact. Thus, invite them to this equalizing resonant tone… of love."

The hearts in the center of the tree, glowed and pulsed. They thumped slowly and deliberately.

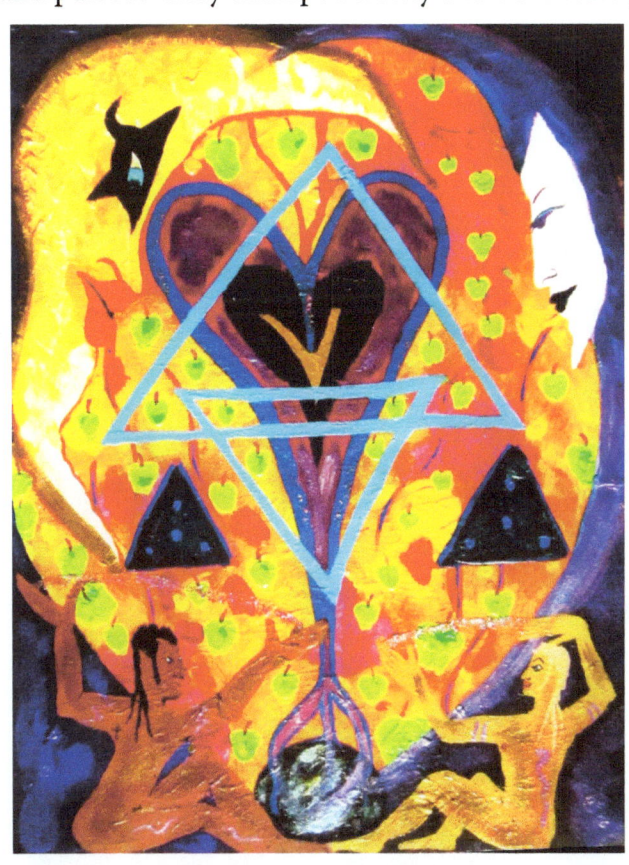

The center is the sun
Surrounded by fun
Where they meet
Is the matrimony of possibilities
Singing octaves, trinities aligned
Three three six twelve
Dimensional tools glow
Organica, equilibrium forms
Addictions declared dead
Golden synchronicity
Validates the crystal grid
Roots in many directions
You are heaven to earth
Knowledge of self and no self
Primed to time and place
Prophesized with change
Ho Ho   Ignite the Sun Chakra ones
Lo Lo, ho ho
Set fire to the frequencies
Activate and liberate the harmonic tones
It is so, It is so, It is so!

The hearts curled up and dropped into the blue sphere that rested between Morgano and Lolaboy. The dream went dark again, and Lolaboy floated into suspended animation for quite some time. Heshe listened to what sounded like a choir of womon singing and the constant dripping of water onto a hard surface.

*I*n this dream, Lolaboy woke in front of a large body of water; perhaps a sea. Morgano was no longer at their side. The jaguar watched as huge animalias swam and leaped above the surface of water. They repeated their acrobatics as if trying to communicate with Lolaboy. Heshe had never had a difficult time understanding the language of any animalia, why now? Something else was strange. Heshe's body had dramatically changed. Lola now had a body like Gaia's, with what looked like a large breast and his organo of masculino was shared with another, that of a feminina, a vuluva. How strange? Heshe examined their new body parts and giggled. What an interesting dream this was going to be!

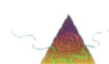

Out of the water leapt a great fish, or what looked like one. However, as Lola focused their eyes, it was a Merstarian. It had been ages since heshe had played with Morgano at the waters' edge with the magical star tribe beings.

"Aho! Lovely Merstarian will you come chat with me?" Lolaboy motioned for them to join heshe on the seashore.

Merstarians were known to be very strange, or rather distant, timid creaturas and rarely shared time with anyone outside their world of oceanica beings. This particular one approached Lolaboy with suspicion. Swimming towards the jaguar magician and then darting away, like someone pulling on a rubber band, only to dive deeper into the depths of the dark blue waters. After a few more times with this dance, the star being emerged from the water with a type of balena, known as an orcata. It jumped into the air and formed a giant circle before it splashed back into the sea.

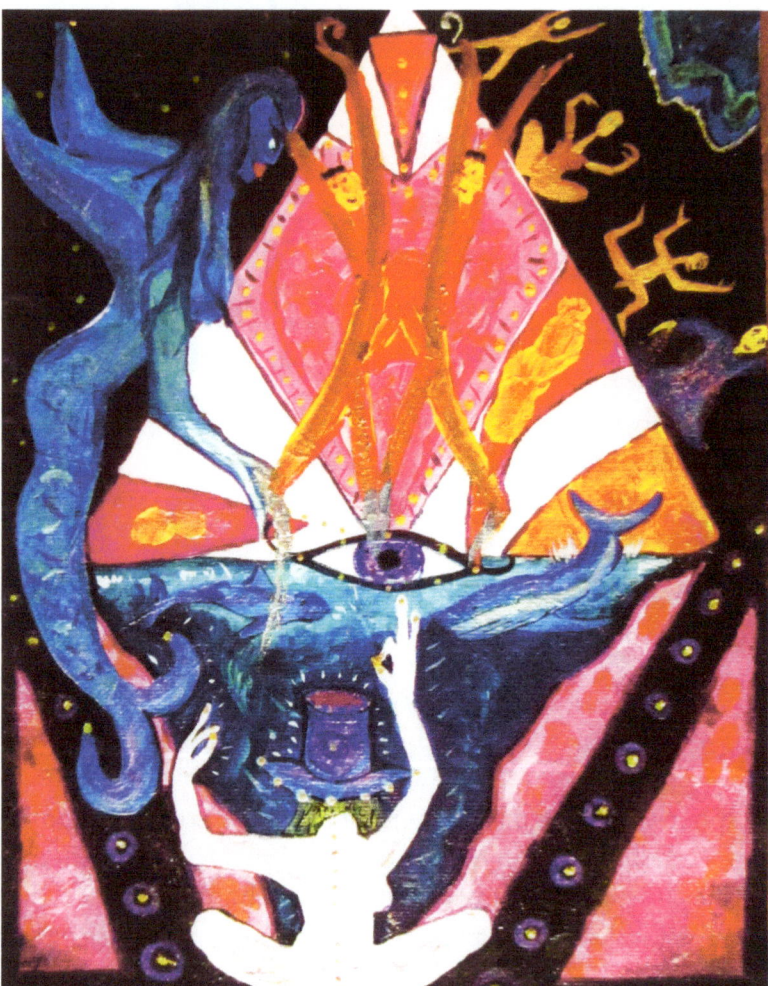

Lolaboy watched as the group swam around and continued to form various shapes leaping from the water's surface into the air and back into its depths. However, after deeper observation, Lola could clearly see what they were doing beneath the water's surface. Heshe could see like a fish!

Without another thought, the Merstarian leaped up so high in the air its shimmering body hovered above Lolaboy and whispered, "Light! Light! Call to myself! Connection to all pathways!" Then she splashed a wave of water so large it drenched Lolaboy.

Lolaboy was confused, but decided to send them thoughts, messages under water. *Balena, I think you are beautiful.*

The whalen responded with a flash of its tail above the surface. It looked like it was waving hello. Lola waved back. *Orcata, what are you and the Merstarian doing?*

In an instant, the orcata swam back and forth pushing large waves that rippled across the surface. One, two, three, four, five, six, seven, counted Lolaboy. Interesting, heshe thought. Isn't seven the number of something I should remember? Vaguely, words of a song returned to Lola's mind. Heshe muttered a view bars,

The sun has the same thoughts as the moon
The moon has the same thoughts as the ocean
The ocean has the same thoughts as the tree...

"And ME," laughed Lolaboy! These are the Aguas de Vida. But, what am I supposed to see in this dream, wondered the jaguar?

At once, orcata dove deep into the depths of the sea until just a whisper of light flickered from their iridescent skin. Within moments, they swam up, up, up and pushed ahead of them thousands of stunning aqua beings of all shapes and sizes. Some of them changed just enough until Lola recognized that they had impressions of heshe's own face on theirs. The cluster of fish split into twelve groups and swam off into the distance until Lolaboy could not longer see them.

Hm… there are twelve of me? Twelve directions, twelve paths! The Merstarian rose up and winked at Lolaboy. Ok… so seven and twelve, I can *see* clearly into the water… um… the fish *are* me. What a puzzle to figure out. It confounded Lolaboy. I'll try something else. Lolaboy raised their hands and formed zeros with heshe's fingers, meditating on an answer. Suddenly the two orcata stuck their heads above the water at the same time. They appeared to have joined their heads to one single body. Perhaps, it was just an illusion created by the water's shiny surface. Hm… *two as one…*? Ah hah! My body… I am two as one, the masculino *and* the feminina in one. The illusion of separateness was no longer. I am zero punta, the place of *center*… cool. I get it, thought Lolaboy.

The Merstarian flapped its tailed excitedly on the top of a wave. Lolaboy looked up at the sky, where there were several golden beings… *humanos… maybe*? The Merstarian flapped her tail again. The golden characters formed their hands in the same way that Lolaboy had done, in the shape of a circle.

Ok… they *see* me. We are *mirroring* each other. It warmed Lola's heart and filled heshe with love. Balena sent a large wave towards the Jaguar, the water rose up, and flowed all around Lola, but strangely they did not get wet.

Hm… something about *responding*, I felt no fear, that was clear. The wave moved around me… I felt *anchored* in my center. Nothing bothers me.

The gold humanos dropped one by one into the sea and swam toward a distant shore. They rose out of the water and walked onto the land. They turned back and pointed to the sky and smiled.

Something was approaching from the sun… The dream went dark.

*W*inds whispered and sounded like distant wailing ghosts. Their moans filled the space with maddening currents. Haunting. Eerie. Lolaboy levitated. Perpetual dreamworld.

In the illusion, Lolaboy witnessed an enormous reflection with heshe's exact features combined with the face of a felina. Heshe sensed that maybe this was the evolved jaguar self. Encircling the fascinating figure were what appeared to be thousands of tiny squares of every imaginable color. The cubes soared into space and created a long spiral path around the double-faced rendering.

"*Who am I?*" Lolaboy queried the daunting vision in front of them.

"It is not the I that makes the self," mocked the mysterious figured? It looked like it could be one of the apparitions known as genias.

"You are *me*," Lola inquired?

"Am I the dreamer being *dreamed*, or the *dreamer* dreaming me?" The being continued to sputter rhetoric, as though it were lecturing to a student.

"I am that I AM," retorted Lola.

"You journey now on the Solina Ribbon of Ilumina. All points are aligned: mastery of instinct, integration of intuition, and knowledge of higher with lower, impulse with action, aspiration with inspiration. This is your magnetic field Lolaboy." The young magician listened vigilantly as heshe observed its lips forming each word. Heshe felt hypnotized.

"Join me on the ascendant master wayseer projection of multiversos. Here we share genuine truth." The spiraling trail twirled in equal rows and columns until the colors synthesized into one; they became vivid white.

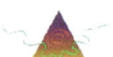

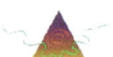

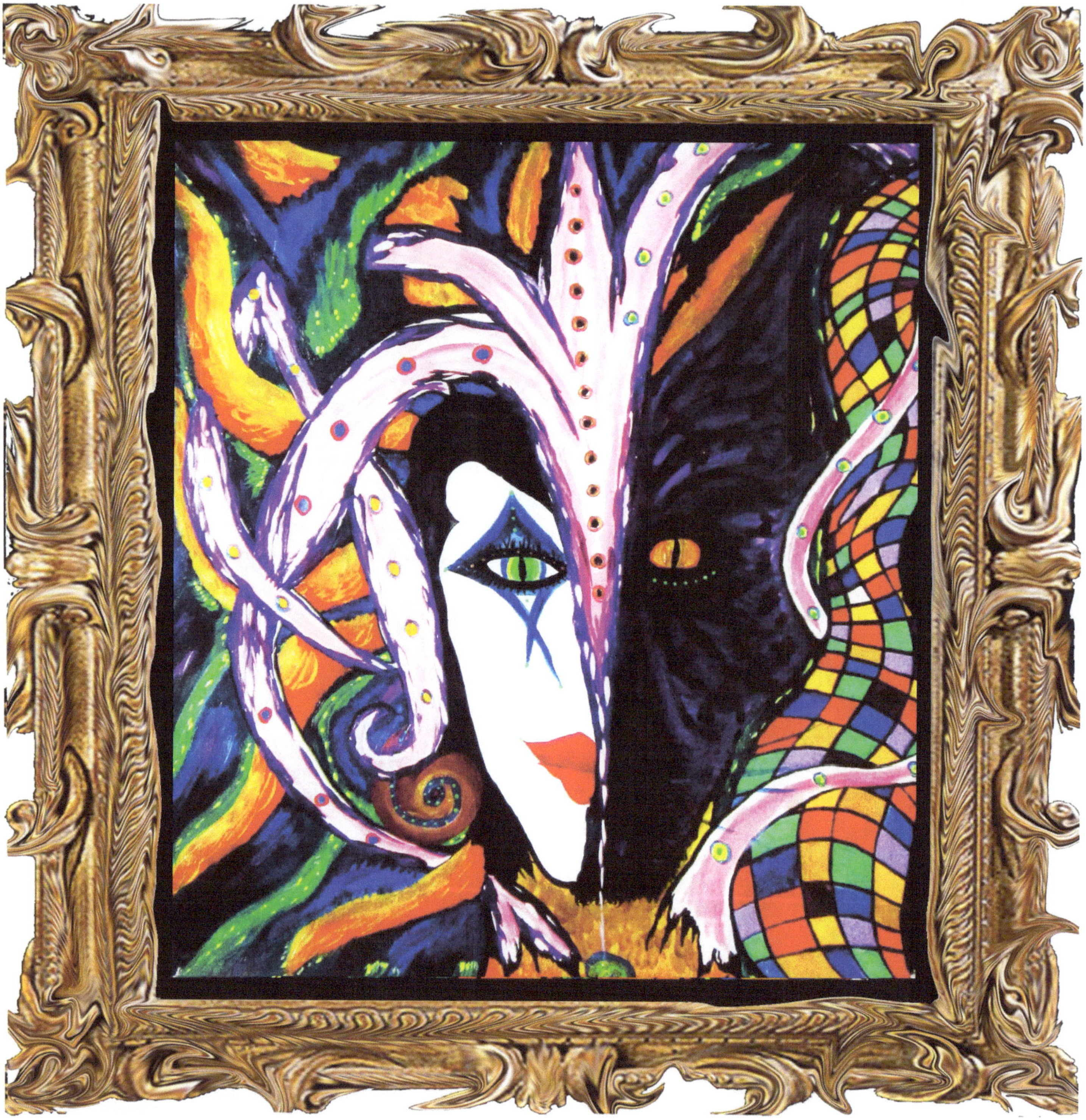

"Celebrate this oneness of selves. Your journey has reached the point of union. All that you have seen, done, or learned has now become one in ecstatic union. This in turn flows out to all points in the universo, reporting on the magic of your mastery. It also has sparked a vortex. Wherever you are, there will now be a pulsating conduit of evolved thought and love. This you shall embody in the day-to-day rhythm on the Planet of Great Consciousness. You are a co-creatrix of the new planeta that soon spans across five dimensionas.

Now, blaze into the infinitum of light where the power of discernment invites you to exhibit refined sensitivity to your environment and innovate new channels of authority. Feed the columns of light on the

c. huilo c.   168 core of the blue planeta with the image of your frequency. Beam your wisdom into the magical grid. Experience this ecstatica and allow it to flow," instructed the vision.

Lolaboy let every bone and muscle relax and drifted away… far away, effortlessly, wondrously into the unknown. Light as a feather, heshe naturally zipped here and there… inside the rainbow of all time. Wistful and magical, the image of the Moon Jaguar was projected onto the sequence of *ah Day eN Ay*. Its celebrated figure was announced to the universo and spectacularly christened into being.

*H*eshe stirred and awoke beneath a lofty pine tree. Shwoo! What dreams I've had, reflected Lolaboy. The young master ruminated over the previous night's visions. After falling asleep, I left Morgano and La Cougera and then passed through quite a whirlpool of revelations. There had been the game with Sun Runner and Muluca, where I had acquired a better understanding of vibrations and shapes. There was the meeting with Payaso Pyneal and the wedding of the hemisfericos with the Sara Belyum. After which, was the unifying of the opposites with Transmuta, and now, what an enlightening dream about the rainbow way.

What would be *next*? One thing, Lolaboy realized, the marriage, this wedding, was about layers of unions, not just *one* as heshe had presumed. The jaguar magician stood up and looked around. They saw a golden glow far off behind a cluster of bushes. Well why not? That *must* be where I go next, Lolaboy grinned. Whatever it is, I am ready to learn more about this marriage and arrive back on the Planet of Great Consciousness. *Soon*, I hope, thought Lolaboy.

Strolling merrily through the woods, the light brightened and greenery popped out everywhere. Spiked ferns, enormous hollyhark bushes, wandering weepy willows curled their leafy branches plunging them forlornly towards the surface of the land, while a few neon gusanos slithered upon the moist ground. Lolaboy sighed with relief and felt connected to everything around, as though it was actually a part of the jaguar's self. Heshe watched a white conehohobunywuny as it hopped behind shrubs. Yes… yes… little one, I know—*fear*. However I no longer feel afraid or even doubtful, crowed Lolaboy to the tree beings. Why *should* I, after everything I've been through? After all, I am participating in one immense dreamtime and always co-creating it. Anyway, why would I choose a feeling I don't *enjoy*?

Something rustled in the bushes next to Lolaboy. Heshe turned and saw a dark silhouette nearly the same height as Lola. "Who are you? Please reveal thyself," demanded Lolaboy. Heshe sensed a lower astral vibration. It felt like the ground had dropped beneath heshe's feet, like an unseen hole had suddenly opened.

"I am another you! The *opposite* of all you know and believe. *Zee zeee… zeeee.* You can't get to me yet, for I live on the Planet of Great Consciousness. But, never mind for now, carry on, silly jaguar. *Zeeee zeeezeeee… heh heeheee.* We are waiting for you jaguar… yes *indeed* we are…" The bushes rattled again and then the shadow disappeared.

Lolaboy trembled. Ok, so I *thought* I wasn't going to feel fear, but that was certainly strange! Heshe shook their head trying to scatter the feeling. Well, whatever that was, it didn't feel good. Hmph. Just when I was feeling ok with everything, Lola sighed.

Small bells tinkled. Lola surveyed the trees for any other strange malicious beings. The distant golden glow was *now* a bright violet. Heshe felt a peculiar urgency and scurried towards the light.

Heshe pushed through some tall reeds and stepped into a clearing. In the center, stood an exquisite looking glass.

"Wow! What a *beautiful* mirror!" Lolaboy admired its ornately carved corners and twisted frame. I wonder if this is the next gate? I must be getting near the last ones, hoped Lolaboy. Heshe's belly tensed.

Lolaboy paced around the mirror. It was much taller than heshe. Of course there were no instructions on how to activate it, *nor* was there anyone around to help. Hmmm, wondered Lola, what am I supposed to do?

Rummaging deep into the pockets of the robes, heshe clasped the key from the Keeper of the Masques. Well? Maybe? Heshe looked around the frame of the mirror and sure enough there was a keyhole. Lolaboy put the key inside, turned it and heard a click, clack. The ground rumbled and then nothing. The magician waited patiently. Nope, nada, nothing else moved, shook or approached.

Heshe reached for the bag of Dusty Miller and blew some of the magical dust toward the mirror. This time the glass appeared to liquefy. The silver surface swirled and turned into a violet myst. Again, Lola waited for something to happen. Heshe put a hand into the violet myst. It felt like a slimy egg. Heshe's arm went inside up to the elbow but no further. Hmmm… Now, let's see… what else can I do? Again, Lola plunged a hand into the protector robes and felt the only thing left… the krystal of clarity. Lolaboy pulled it out and held it up, once again admiring its stunning opalescence. Heshe noticed in one of the tiny facets on the gem, there were three letters. *I, A, M.* Of course! I *am*! Laughing hysterically, heshe had come full circle and arrived to the same mirror where Morgano had introduced them to the Zuvuyana, the grandmother aracnia.

"Who am I? *I am that I am of the I am,*" shouted Lolaboy!

Just as the last *am* rolled off heshe's tongue, bells clanged, violet mysts turned emerald green and sprayed from the mirror. A hollow metallic sound joined the chorusas while someone plucked a violinia.

Power now
Balanced with love
Oh sacred marriage
Magnetic protectors
Illumine the wisdome
The truth beyond the polarities

The Jaguar has Come!
The Jaguar has Come
Indeed, the Moon Jaguar!

Inside the feminina
Outside the masculino
Union of contraries
Enlightened rainbow
Sacrament you are!

The Jaguar is here!
The Jaguar is here!
Moon Jaguar has arrived!

Purified and regenerated
Trust and belief
Discrimination and complements
Justice and secrets
Regenerate you have!

Now, come inside
Resurrect you have
Moon Jaguar!

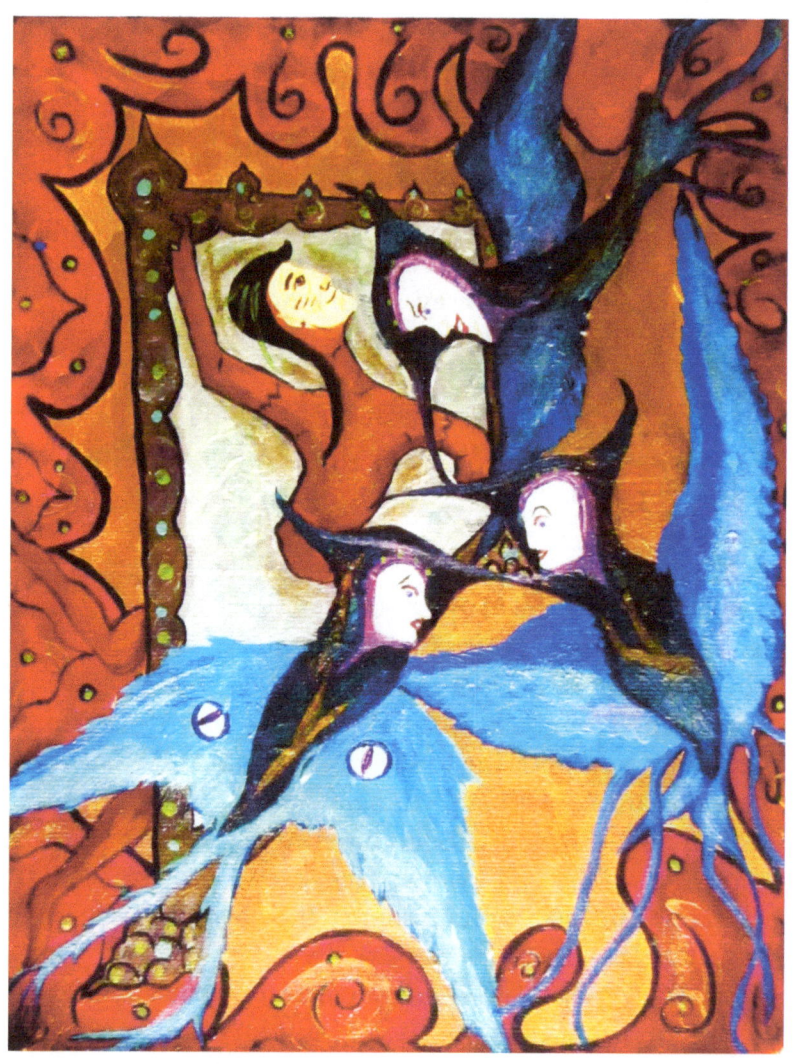

c. huilo c.

In the core of the mirror a dark hole formed. Lolaboy jumped with joy and dove into the orifice. Heshe was sucked deep into its depths, further and further, swirling madly… various images appeared here and there, a sword, another mirror, a staircase, and then, there was a *skyskraper*! Suddenly, whoosh… and Lolaboy was pulled out by the Flower Kissers!

"Teeeeheheheheee. Teeeeeheheheheeee. Tee Teee Teee. Ooooo welcome moon jaguar, Lola indeed. Welcome again to the golden realm!" The Flower Kissers buzzed around spraying a sweet juice and dampening Lolaboy's black hair with medicina alegre.

"What a journey! How wonderful to see you all again! Ho! Ho!" Lolaboy leaped and pranced like an antelope with such exuberance that even the Flower Kissers had difficulty following the jaguar. Heshe danced madly, wondrously, mesmerized by the completion of the *adventurer's quest*. This must mean that I am ready to go and awaken the other two spirits, hoped Lolaboy.

"Tee teee teee. We strengthen you with harmony and tranquility and once again you arrive on the Path of Great Beauty." The Flower Kissers continued to swirl around Lolaboy. They moved so quickly Lolaboy could no longer distinguish their shapes. Where the birds had just been emerged a gigantic crystalina form. Not only that, out heshe's back grew wings again! Lolaboy took flight and headed, with great curiosity, to the giant gem. Lola continued spinning around in glee. Never mind that the Flower Kissers had disappeared, all was in ecstatic union.

---

*C*harged with so much energy Lolaboy flew swiftly into the enormous crystalline.

Lolaboy, Lolaboy Lolaboy
The earthstar calls your name
Conflict still is here
Separation, doubt and delusion
Fear of the unknown

Lolaboy Lolaboy Lolaboy
Your time is near
Release, separation, control
Deception and complacency
No more! No more!

Lolaboy Lolaboy Lolaboy
Amplify your spirit at this time
Many faceted creatura you are
Imagine your self here
8:8 11:11 12:12 13:20

Spheric core of color
Vibrational harmony of will
Brilliant diamond of clarity
Carry your consciousness now
Lola! Lola! Lola!

During the excitement heshe's veins surged with life, Lola plunged into the giant column that summoned. However, something else tugged at Lolaboy. While grabbing heshe's cloak, as fast as the desire to get to the krystal, heshe was simultaneously filled with apprehension and grief. What would I do when I arrived on the planeta? Then, abruptly, Lolaboy plummeted and fell away from the pulsing gem.

"Psssst... pssst... Lolaboy, it's me, La Cougera. I'm going to send you someone to help with this resistance. Look beneath you, she's coming. Ciminian, the Bridger of Worlds. It seems that part of you is still being churned about on the rainbow ribbon. This lovely member, of the Tribe of Equus, has offered to escort you back to the auric realm of Gaia." La Cougera raised her pearl cloak and swirled it lively into the air. At once she was soaring in the air next to Lolaboy. "I will accompany you."

"Thank you, I don't know *what* overcame me," moaned Lolaboy.

"I think you *do* know, but we can discuss that later. For now, I'll use my ability to face the unknown. It was gifted to you from the master, Pumana Peakok. She waved a scepter over Lolaboy's head.

Soon after, Ciminian arrived. The centaur kneeled and offered its arched back to Lolaboy. "Hop on! We have an appointment, a reunion set to do some magia!" La Cougera smiled radiantly at Lolaboy while heshe flew off with Ciminian.

The two raced into the atmosphere towards the revolving krystal, which had now sprouted two smaller versions of itself from midpoints on either side. Above the gems there had formed a phantom-like image. It was Gaia. To her side were images, one of a jaguar, and the other was a humano. Two other guests had arrived, one from the east, and one from the west. Transmuta, who had gorgeous plumage now, flew with them across the celestial space, joined by la Cougera and Lolaboy.

After they arrived, they lingered over the gemstone. Inside its center, where the two pyramided facets joined, was the Planet of Great Consciousness. It was astonishingly beautiful as it revolved slowly on its axis. Sparkling and turning, the blue planeta shined in its amazing glory.

Gaia addressed the group. "Welcome masters of these times. Bakal of the Western Wirld, you bring the waters of new dreams, thank you. And, you, Nakan of the Eastern Wirlds, have brought the kernels of new beginnings, thank you. La Cougera, Lolaboy and Transmuta, I am humbled to have you join me in this ritualia immersion where we shall fuse energies to the auric realm of my dear offspring, the Planet of Great Consciousness." Gaia gazed serenely down at the krystal, which emcompassed the Planet.

"What a gorgeous manifestation Geominizer conjured for us. It is the Octehedronal of Reconciliashun. Indeed, it is a Diamante of Gloria. Now... together we must focus our intent and will upon the planeta to prepare itself for the massive shift of intelligence. It shall begin to engage and receive the reharmonization of the vibrations and release the bampirica sinistros that have sabotaged the organic freedom of humanos." Gaia addressed her friends from within a large red pyramid.

Each of them began to resonate a tone. They chanted and hummed willingness and wonder into the Diamante of Gloria.

Now, I hereby call forth the Path of *Ah Day eN Ay* to restore itself in all beings of all realms who now reside upon, within or near the Planet of Great Consciousness. I ask it to restore the codigos of Universal blueprint of Absolute Love. I invite it to restore wellbeing to the Origin of Life."

Each of the guests echoed, "A Ho! A lo ha! A lah! A hah! A mayne! Ah!" They repeated each verse as Gaia chanted.

"I call upon the energies of masculino, feminina and the Unifying Principles of Wholeness."

The tones reverberated back and forth across the heavens. Lolaboy watched with the others as the Diamante of Glory burst open and the *ah Day eN Ay* began to spiral through the Planeta.

"Enter the 12 Pentacles, the 60 facets, the 72 truncations and double yourself to the rhythm of 144, thus entering the realm of Merkababa! We invoke the Patternas of Paz upon all bridges forming alliances with this planeta now and from here on! Amplify now the Balance of the electrical channels that charge and attract the nature of empathic joy!" Gaia opened her eyes wide and glared at the blue planeta. She knew it was a vulnerable time for the Planet of Great Consciousness to open its core essence. However, she alsoknew that nothing else could be done in order to avoid more ruthless tendencies that continued to magnetize and create massive destruction. Even with all this focus from her allies, the total change of the vibratory realms on a planeta takes time. It would also require the assistance of elevated humanos. Would Lola be able to reflect this energy—and soon enough? While doubt could never cloud the matrix of thought within a divine being, nothing was for certain in the universo.

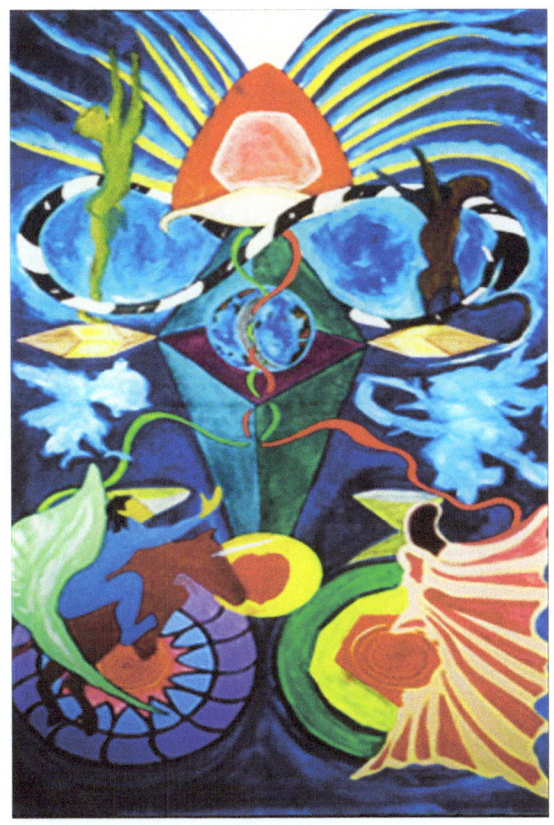

While the dynamic team assembled by Gaia continued to energize awareness into the filaments on the core of the Planet of Great Consciousness, others tended to it behind the scenes with critical tasks.

Ocelotl strolled though the deep woods with Whitelionmeetswhitebuffalowoman. They arrived at a copper cauldron. The large bowl sat upon the Rock of Ages.

"We must call upon Tellurusious. It is better to have three of us here to perform the necessary ritual for calling upon the Akashicanical Libraries. We need to invoke many more tools to support Gaia's effort along with the others. Their crucial attempt to repair the fabric of knowledge around the planeta may work just by itself. However, I believe we must come to aid and assist in breaking of the Shields of Menace. Perhaps Fuego will also join us?"

Whitelion roared. The booming voice exploded through dense woodland and swiftly parted the clouds. Lightening bolts zigzagged and hit the ground. The electrical rays ignited a fire under the Cauldron of Manifestation.

The fire blazed and bellowed. "Ocelotl, I have come. It is I, Fuego, of the Elementals. I am determined to fuel and launch the Portal of Possibilities."

"Thank you kindly, dear elemental. Well done. We've quite a mission ahead. Even those of us that know there is no inherent right nor wrong, there is the potential of malicious outcome in the vast array of the universo. As you know, it's our heart's desire to stabilize this utterly astounding and unique form of consciousness within Gaia's realm. Certainly, without a doubt, whatever we cast here with our will shall add

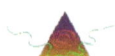

to the bloom of positive magia now swirling in the ethers. Hopefully our effort will contribute to the volatile fluctuation of the grid templates around the planeta. In many ways, we know it's better sometimes not to know the risks, thereby we can wholeheartedly contribute to the cause. In reality only free will of the humanos can change their circumstance… I think that goes without explanation."

The cauldron spit and sputtered, and boiled and fizzed a bluish froth. Fuego licked the sides of the bowl as it continued to cook. The mixture of consciousness brewing in the center of the masters started to form different layers. A spume of bubbles rose to the top while gelatinous ooze sank to the bottom. The alchemy had begun.

"Ah yes… we see the strata of the records forming. Now, once we separate them, and retone them with honor we must rejoin them as well. After that, we shall seal them with the Golden Capstone. This will firmly attach the series of actions that Gaia and the others perform. We send it forth with the desire for maximum success to humanos. Through a series of well-intended actions, we make it so! For the greater good of all beings in the Universo, the Planet of Great Consciousness, and the jaguar magicians!"

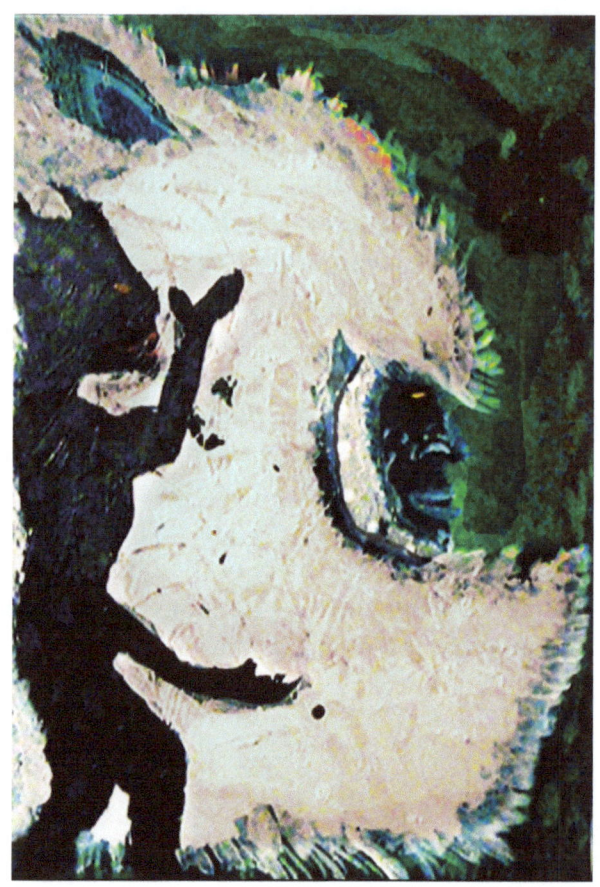

Together they declared out loud, "It is done! It is done! It is done!"

$\mathscr{O}$celotl reached into the Cauldron of Manifestation and pulled out a scroll of papeyereesh. He untied it and rolled it out onto the moss-covered ground. Whitelionmeetswhitebuffalowoman studied it along with the jaguar magician. In the document, a hazy image began to move about the surface. It was Tellurusious.

"Dear ally, we are in deep gratitude for your assistance. As Gaia's counter essence, the story of humanos resides within your dominion as well. Is this diagram we have in front of us the one that shares the sequential stargates to the Meta-tronia Channel," Ocelotl inquired?

"Brother, it is as you say. I reveal the direction for the Golden Mean Spiral. As you know, these are the purified codigos for the expression of heavenly awareness." Tellurusious pointed to a chasmia in the chart.

"This is an unstable separation. It has fueled much of the disruption. Indeed, here is the ancient future you referred to… of how Gaia's realm might become a location for the lesson of opposites. However in spite of this original intention, it has attached to itself and the separation spasms out of control."

Whitelion paced and contemplated details in the chart. "May I join you inside the Akashicanical record? I think, while Ocelotl assists from the outside, I would like to biolocate inside the navigation records. Together we can adjust and move around a few of the stargates."

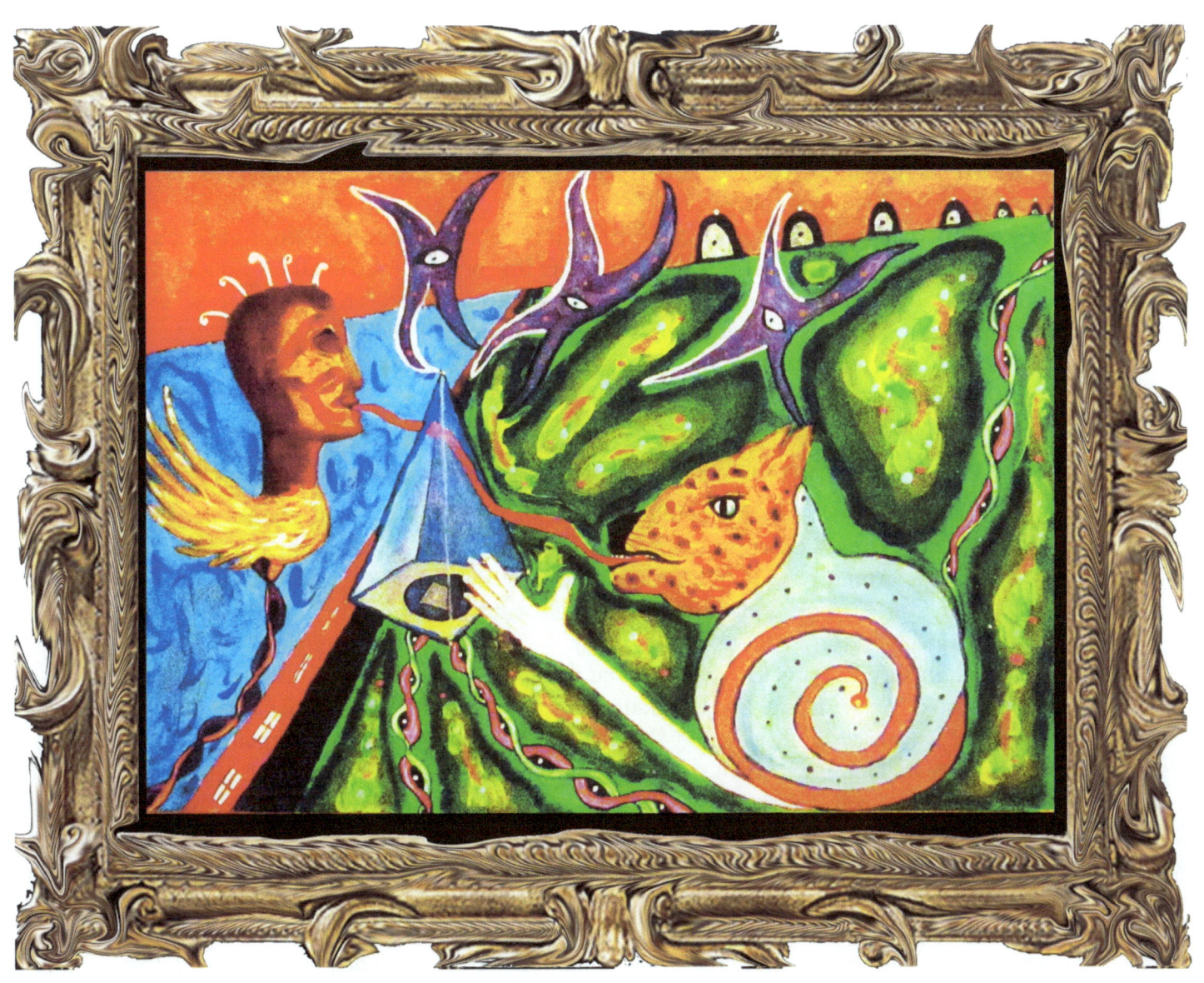

"Of course master Lion, I hereby invite you into the realm that is the Dominion of Tellurusianos. Welcome! Here! Here!" Tellurusious opened the channel and Whitelion appeared majestically upon the field of consciousness.

Three unusual purple leaf-like shapes popped into existence. "These are coded with the light of our will. I shall summon the Prime Mistikal Virtues. You, justice! You, integrity! You, hope! And the rest… empatica, faith and willingness come forth and fill this chasm of disruption! Onto this playing field I call upon your names and summon your vibration to flow," bellowed the Whitelion.

Ocelotl called forth a string of the *ah Day eN A* that spread from Gaia's work on the blue planeta. "Feed this strand into the channel. We can direct it through the separation into the stargates on the horizon."

"Activate stargates: Shadow! Duality! Shift! Transformation! Along with that — myth, dream and transcendence!" Whitelion and Tellurusious began to build a bridge that formed a path for the new language of light to cross the canal.

Ocelotl waved his paw and a tetrahedron formed. He positioned the *ah Day eN A* through the channel and formed a four-sided pyramid.

"With the will of all reverent beings we call forth and restore the natural rhythms of Gaia's animism, because it is with her belief, and ours, that the diversity of life that once thrived shall blossom again on this noble blue planeta. Through our cooperation we congeal the intentions and form a new legend to be created for the humanos to flourish within their true, heart-knowing essence," hailed Ocelotl!

The ground rocked, rumbled, and rattled. Trees swayed back and forth, while gale force winds sent the intentional violet leaves flying into the stargates.

By now, it seemed everything was stirring in the Universo. In some way the Creators were also drawn into the tale of the Planet of Great Consciousness. The bells of the sacred reunion, the marriage of the opposites had notified the furthest reaches of time and space that significant changes were occurring with possibilities on the holografica lattice. Indeed, by the will of the tribal unions, the architectural projections were converting space at all levels.

Once Lolaboy had finished the ritualia with Gaia and the others, heshe asked if it was possible to take a reprieve in the Enchanted Forest. Heshe had dramatically changed from their experience of integrating such strong magic. While Lola was certainly elated by the majesty of the practice, something had also become alarmed by the exposure to the immensity of such forces.

The power of intention or will… heshe wondered if it could be directed at negative thoughts as well? What would that do? The shadows plagued Lolaboy. Heshe spent a few nights wandering endlessly in the forest seeking a clue to cure this growing ill will. Temptations triggered anxiety. It felt like there was a ghost lingering next to the young magician. Lolaboy sensed a strong tug at their heart and dropped next to a thickly barked tree. It was spiney and irritated heshe's back. It seemed there was nowhere comfortable to rest.

The woods bowed their limbs and sent waves of healing to Lolaboy. They helped heshe work through the difficulty until its impact was diminished. There was a rustle in the leaves. Crunch, crunch popped the dry leaves as someone approached Lolaboy. Next to the trunk of a nearby tree emerged a stunning lizard being.

"DreamWeaver! How are you my friend," asked Lolaboy, somewhat glumly?

"I am as agitated as you are… It seems *everything* is changing. Ocelotl and the others are completely involved with high rites though I personally prefer to be still and watch, you know, dream. However, my dear jaguar, that tone you have, Lola, I recognize it. It's curious and also somewhat foreboding. I wonder of all this glory and if it also isn't time to address the strengthening of polarities and their offspring.

While many of your guardians and guides have been invoking astonishing goodwill on your journey, there have been other forces participating in your growth as well. Some refer to this energy as the Enorganicots and the Bvamperica, those that desire to deter the evolushun of good will."

"I don't know what it is DreamWeaver, but something is lurking in me, around me… I feel possessed at times by this violent energy. I just wish I could understand it better. It's more than the ability to integrate the selves or even shifting my thoughts, I feel that… But what have I yet to grasp?" Lolaboy wanted terrifically to understand the way the universo existed and what had *really* happened on the Planet of Great Consciousness…

"Ah, well, this is a good start. Wonder… Well, perhaps it's time to summon a council then, and we can discuss the temptation and seduction of power, emotions, even the inability to participate in one's complete destiny. There are many things to ponder." DreamWeaver rose up on his hind legs and made a low bellow and then a series of high pitched barks.

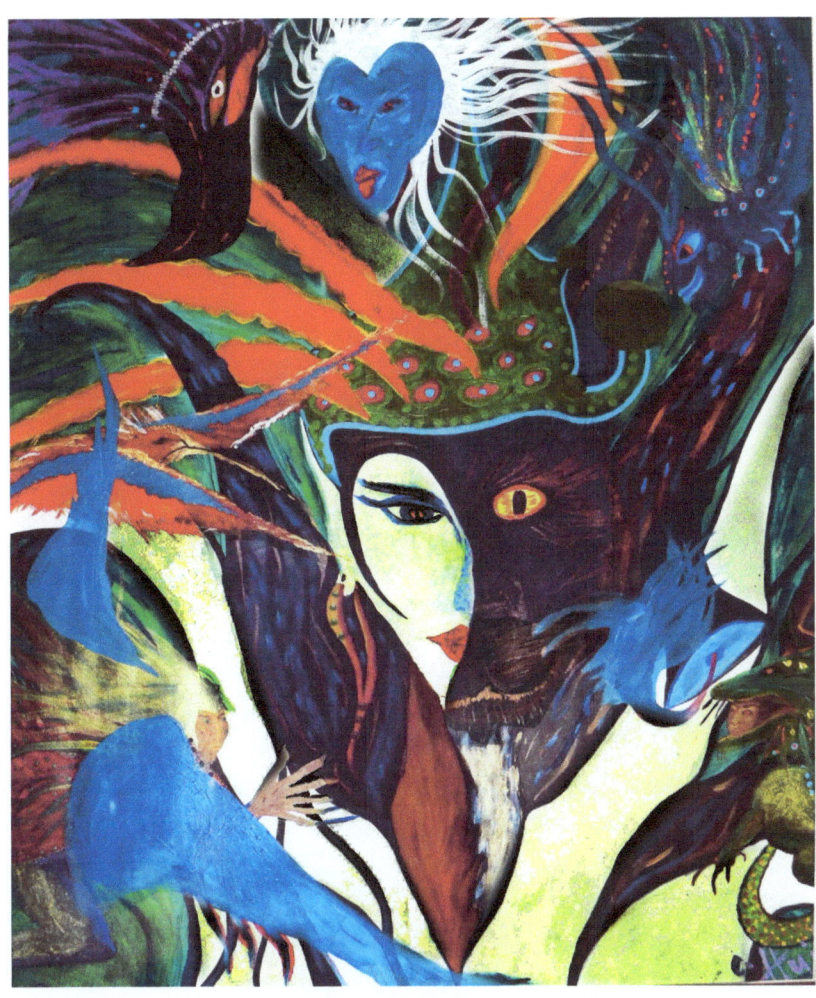

Wither nither lunderloo
Who wants to be the crew?

Hither thither bundercoo
Join us under the darkening moon?

Slither blither, hunderdoo
We call upon the masters of the loon…

The two waited in silence. The stillness was unnerving. The boughs of the trees began to swish and wail like banshees. Then the sound of rushing water, perhaps it was a cascade falling from the side of a nearby mountain, or perhaps it was…

"Lavishingly luring us again with your sexy croons?" A petite winged creatura fluttered from the canopy of trees. "Greetings Lolaboy, DreamWeaver."

"I think we've met? Are you the blueberry faerie?" asked Lolaboy shifting to look closely at the newly arrived guest.

"No… no… that one's a distant cousin, I'm more *closely* related to Durkata. I come from the school of Mastery in Mysterious Mischievous Menacing Methods, MMMMM, for short!" snickered the pixie. "But some call me Pixy Puranono. Though, perchance, it may be that we are the *same* being… blueberry and me! However, this council you call forth… it interests me DreamWeaver. Indeedy doo it does."

DreamWeaver shushed the two and pointed to the center of the clearing. Sprouting from the ground, a purple vine pushed up from the leaves and continued to grow until it was more than 5 feet tall. Thin leaves formed on either side of the stem. It developed a large bell shaped bud that sadly drooped from a stem. The counsel watched as the sprout slowly opened into an exquisitely deep indigo colored trumpet shaped bloom. The flower blossomed and swayed from side to side as if it were sizing the two up.

"Hey there…I'm Orchida Negra, Flora of the Nethera Terrano. Lizard being, I have also heard your call and wish to participate in your assembly. Doubt we not that all worlds and realms are shuddering with the reports transmitted through the ethers these days?" The flower emitted a fragrant myst into the air.

"Ah, night blossoming one, good of you to come. There is one other who has also arrived. Look up there…" DreamWeaver pointed to the treetops. A striking raptor was just folding its strong wings. It had arrived silently… the bird was the incredibly mystifying and wondrous, it was Phoenix. Its sharp beak opened and sang,

Council of the naught
Hallowed haunts in the fissures
Time awaits noone

Inspiring inquiries of the lurking lots
We gather into the lures
Wondering of the ways

Creep not in matera dimness
One only needs to observe
From there all wait

The daunting bird flapped its great wings and moved to a limb closer to the circle. At the same time the others continued to brood on their nocturnal pursuits.

It's your imagination
Creatures of the night
Everything is going very smoothly here
You must be getting confused

"What are those creepy whispers in the woods?" Lolaboy looked around and sank into their place on the ground. Lola was increasingly uncomfortable with everything.

Come with us
We have a future
For more than you want
Just the very thought of it
Use your imagination

"Pay them no mind," hushed DreamWeaver. "They're the one's we speak of, the Enorganicots and the Bvampira. Do not afford them any of your attention." The lizard walked to the edge of the clearing and circled the space deliberately, chanting quietly. While nevertheless, the voices continued to provoke them,

Why ignore what doesn't fit into your mind
Bahahahahahaa
You who think you know it all
Dancers of the night!
Way to the new world
Tee. hee. hee. hee.
Indeed.

Orchida Negra puffed more of her magical perfume myst into the atmosphere. "That should quiet them for a bit. Oh little jaguar, once there, that dear planeta… oh my, the rifts and gaps between here and there are so large, and dare I say, seemingly ominous. In any case, here… take this." She handed Lolaboy a vial of liquid. "It's the essencia of my nectar. You may use anytime the finitum tries to overpower you with a tendency for melancholy."

"Thank you kindly. I am sure I will be fine." Lolaboy turned to the lizard, "But, DreamWeaver, are any others coming to this council? I'd like to learn as much as I can about these stirrings I have inside me, around me. These voices in the woods, *anything* you can share." Lolaboy glanced up at the Phoenix. Once upon a time, heshe was filled with delight at its sight, but even now the bird of paradise seemed to hint at the complexity of the tasks before all of them. There was an air of caution around the council that evening.

"Very well, then, I'll do my best. It's interesting that you, Pixy Puranono, have joined us. I hope you can offer some skills to Lolaboy… for deterring the effects of mischievous ministries that prevail on the planeta?" DreamWeaver ambled into the center of the camp and looked around carefully, nodding to each of the members of the council.

"Well, perhaps, I'll begin with a dream I just had. In it, I heard a sound, it made me frown. I looked around and at the ground. There were two little birds. Feet up and head down. Colors spilt upon the mound. Menacing to find. It nearly left me blind. I turned them over. Pink like a clover. Their flight was gone. Soon it would be dawn. Wandering into the night. Thick with fright. Wings spread out. They gave a shout. Bliss kiss frail. Run for the pail. Pour the waters. And raise the daughters." DreamWeaver stood frightenly still, as if in a trance.

Lolaboy, Pixy and Orchida waited for DreamWeaver to continue, but the Lizard stood in dead silence. Pixy jumped up, prattled and pranced about while mumbling some sort of gibberish.

"Wyst nyst qnewt, hackjak cuspat neeloggin." The Pixy flew up to a low branch. "Pisht. Your dreams. DreamWeaver. They make no sense to me! Do you think *this* helps? It's useless."

"Well then, what have you to offer proud sprite? Pixy prattle?" DreamWeaver left the center and retreated to the side.

"I can offer this! That while we sit here proposing to help the anxious jaguar magician, the mix thickens. Dense it is… with layers of thought and fabrication of whimsy and wallabaloo. Lolaboy, listen to me. Dare I say, nay are the planetary wirlds. Tossed about, broken apart, destroying themselves? Rising and spilling their contents into the universo. Our world is but a fantasy to them. Humanos have been cursed! Afflicted with despicable notions about the Ways of Awakening. Lazy and annoying they are to me, whilst you all sit here in glee. Stubborn those peepul are… irritating me with their ignorance. Why does their resulting behavior impale this council? Because everything everywhere in all the tyme is *connected*! And just that!" Pixy flew off in a zany mixture circles and nose dives, flashing about above the council. The sprite continued to mutter in gibberish.

Deeper and deeper we go

                              Shouldn't they know?

      Truth of the eternal

                                      Desire to the presumptuous foes?

Heaving a hefty blast of fragrant spray into the air another time, Orchida Negra stated boldly, "You! Whatever congeals the Matrix of Doubt! Dense as you are, the Universo knows nothing of itself at all! Thereby, gathering even from the distant haunts, beyond the wildest idea, from the vastness and the emptiness, the nothingness and the everythingness… grows and grows the fervent imagination of care… of Absolute Love."

"Willy nilly silly bloom. That's what I say! What is this love of suffering, hey? Ney, you bring the wrath of pleasant, gest you with the swarm of positivity and forget the chaos of it all? Myopic entropic phobia them all! Nee thee welcome the onslaught of the enormity of separation that caused it all?" Puranono flittered to one side of the clearing and then dashed to the other. "I say! What is this council of egos?"

Winds. They came in swiftly. Light at first, then gathering force, shaking the leaves one by one, then by the tens, until there was a blinding storm of debris. The four of them huddled together and took cover.

"Bas Tach Ix Tal Men!" The Phoenix raised its mighty wings and the winds quickly subsided. The enormous raptor took flight and circled the sky above the circle three times and landed with a whoosh. The bird closed one of its eyes and began to speak.

"Young Lola. DreamWeaver. Orchida Negra. Pixy Puranono. Grace upon the ground you gather. The Great Mystery has birthed every one of us! Producing facets and layers, parallel and twin, the Ultimos Universos cannot be explained. Fractures bring the chance for this illogical mass to know thy self. Humanos separated from the patterns of which we converse. Once on the planeta, Lola, you *must* consider these universal decrees... for the Planet of Great Consciousness continues to turmoil... while we attend to the affairs called into being by the Creators... remember the wisdom which furthered your cause aided by various sentinels and professors:

The responsibility of ideas has become incongruent withn the greater good of Gaia's child.

The very conjuring of waking dreams creates menacing tangible forms.

The division into layers upon their axis of consciousness has brought about disequilibrium in the characteristics of the gender categories.

Their ability to sense the subtlety of the all that ever was has been weakened and their will has been tainted by immense disruptive behaviors.

A process of regeneration is underway.

Holografica designs are spawning new lattices of event construction

The lesson was formed to observe the polaric fields which integrate opposing sides until they again are restored to unity.

The miraculous bird raced off into the night sky and left the four members of the council in a contemplative silence.

"Well, that said and done, I'm off, Lolaboy, when you arrive to that loco dimenshun again, contemplate what the Phoenix offered. And I will add this, take nothing too much to heart as your experience of it all is yours and yours only. Hold a state of observation with neutrality. Thereby, you may walk serenely through their gates of deluded attempts and commanding power over the sagrado laws of Gaia's realm. Indeed, should the illusions tempt you to lose your faith, drink of the beauty in her surrounding mysts. While the throbbing rocks wobble to reform, you can, just by being there, stabilize the vigor and vitality of the original dream for humanos. Go forth!" Pixy Puranono flapped his transparent wings and disappeared deep into the woods.

Lolaboy sighed. "I thought this would make it easier. *Knowing*."

"Eh, knowing is intriguing, and sometimes the *unknowing* of what you think you know is even *more* interesting and nourishing. Wondrous jaguar, I bow to you. I share with you, that as you hear my voice, and you speak with the lot of us, the ones on the planeta, their story, no doubt, will always live in a infinitum. While they clutch to the finitum, I wish you well on your exploration! Sadly, we are mere objectifications to many who live there now. Something only from a myth or textbook. Certainly, there are those who feel a tingle here and there with the memory of our conversations from ancient future pastimes. Oh how I bliss you. Remember, while you will hear the flora on the planeta speak, the others may not…at least for a short time longer… they are deaf… as that rift is about to be joined again." The flower curled its petals and a couple of them fell to the ground. "Alas, nothing is as it seems forever. Even I am to wither and transform, here on this spot. To a memory, a place of once upon a time… Lovely Lolaboy, travel well." The stem, leaves and flower shriveled up and withered to the ground.

Only Lola and DreamWeaver remained in the forest clearing… For a long time they sat and enjoyed the stillness. Then a dim, purple light filled the clearing. Lolaboy looked up. The moon was rising.

"*H*ey! Lighten up! It's me Luna Oscuro!" The new moon shined its light directly above where the council had gathered. He lowered himself in the sky and beamed a lovely lavender glow upon the forest clearing.

A deep sigh came from Lolaboy. DreamWeaver stood on all four legs and sauntered to the edge of the clearing.

"Lolaboy, I must retreat now. Perhaps, none of this made sense… Even so, most importantly, remember your light within. The joy of the Flower Kissers. This ambiguity you may feel is actually the splendor and the attraction of your willingness to question. One day, I'll meet you again in dreamtime while you traverse that remarkable blue planeta… So long." The lizard vanished into the thick trees.

"Hi Luna. Well, how are things in *your* world," snickered Lolaboy? "I really like that lizard, since I first met him in the Enchanted Forest. He's *so* mellow."

"Surely, that he is. Well…well! You've come such a long way. Oh dear friend, let all this knowingness wash away for a moment. Enjoy the luminosity of this night while I offer you a soothing song."

Hmmmm oh how the veils shall release
Hmmmmm oh how harmony fills the dell
Hmmmm oh now is the time to spell

Living in the golden shape
Raise your purple shimmering cape
Rising high rising high up up you go…

Lolaboy began to rise into the sky next to Luna Oscuro. The moon continued to sing,

Oooooh wonder of it all
There never could be a fall
Let us go spin the wondrous ball

Hmmmm mmmmmm hmmmmm mmmmmm

Lolaboy and the moon soared across the heavens. After awhile they reached a place where below them, the blue planeta drifted on her seemingly relentless journey. The Planet of Great Consciousness swirled with all of its daunting blue, white and turquoise wisps. Luscious aquas, sapphires, cerulean and indigo, the colors blended into a mass orb of wonder. This dominion of Tellurusious and the humanos was undergoing massive changes. It would imprint the entire universo with the story of what it became, its possibility, and subsequently the outcome would dance tendencies for all future worlds.

"Well hello there dear ones." Zuvuyana joined Luna Oscuro and Lolaboy. Hanging by a silk thread she swung towards them. "Shall we do a little repair work," chuckled the elder aracnia?

"What a good idea. Lola, you can help!" Luna dropped down and pulled up a transparent, silver layer of mesh from the planeta. "This is a membrano. There are a number of these auric tiers around the planeta. And… as you can see this one has some slashes in it."

"Nothing a little weaving can't fix." Grandmother spider picked up part of the membrano and began to interlace fine silken strands. "Now, what shall we sing into the weave? Or chant? Invocation? Some think they're the same. Not really though, you see the manner of the tones create a different resonance."

"Why don't we put innocence into it," Lolaboy offered?

"Well, what a good idea! And so we shall… innocence with…hmm… a touch of eloquence? That may increase ability to integrate new ways of expression. What would you like to add my dear Luna?" The spider continued zigzagging, pulling strings here and there across the membrano.

The moon contemplated her offer then proposed, "Let's spin intuition and instinct into this fabric of consciousness, and a whole lot of fun, eh? It gets a bit serious down there…"

Itza mitza mobbly moo
Judging and categorizing you do
Sprinkle splatter plop
Let us take up the mop

And spin spin spin
Itza mitza mobbly moo

Creating a new din
That the rebellious rise up
And protected they are

And spin spin spin
Itza mitza mobbly moo

Spiral into this we do
Innocence, intuition and influence
Spiral this we do

And spin spin spin
Itza mitza mobbly moo!

Release these densities within a flash
Fear and poverty clash
Off they go in a dash!

And spin spin spin
Itza mitza mobbly moo!

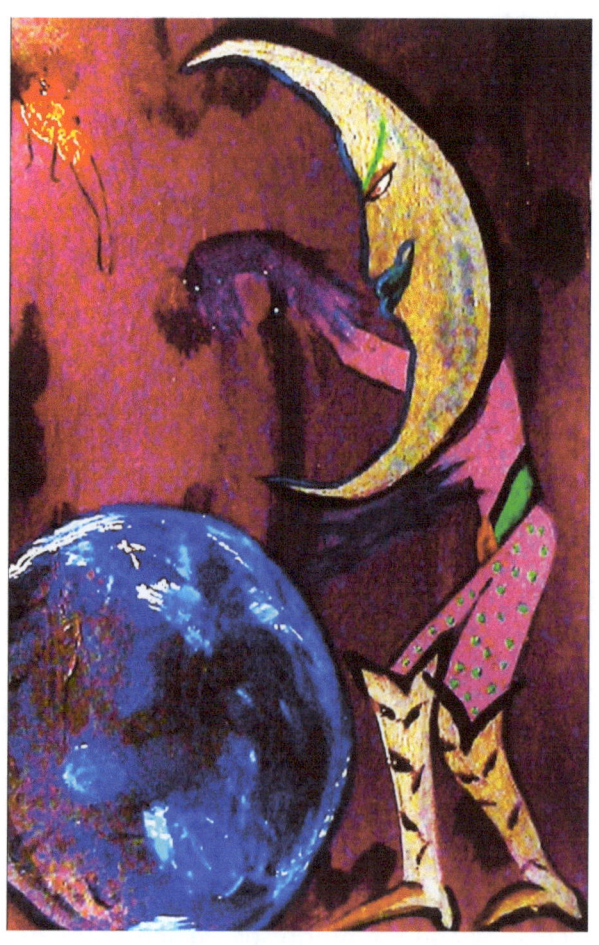

*A*fter the three weavers of the night finished their repairwork on the membrano, Lola left them and returned to the forest one more time. Luna had informed heshe that the marriage was soon to be sealed and that there were only a couple more rites. He advised Lola that the time to engage the mastery of the gates and mirrors was soon to come and the re-entry to the finitum terrano of the planeta would happen almost immediately afterwards.

Lolaboy found a large tree near a brook and sat mindlessly humming a soft lyrical tone. Heshe enjoyed the serenity of the woods, and now that the journey through the Carnival of Souls was near completion, Lola thought it was a good time to reflect. That young Lola of La Selva was now a weaver alongside Zuvuyana and the Lunas, and heshe had even participated in sacred rites with La Cougera and Morgano. Now it would be heshe's task to mirror and illumine these characteristics onto other jaguar magicians and humanos living on the planeta. Lolaboy felt confident that the impact of all the guardians and guides would dramatically alter the etherical realms. Heshe knew they could assist on the quest and thus Gaia's realm would increase its vibration. How all this would result, it would be *anyone's* guess.

Heshe now understood the path to change locations at will and would share as much wisdome without judgment to the others on the planeta. After all, everyone was a divine twin to some degree and any separation that might try to seduce the jaguar could be dissolved by free will… the willingness to re-member. By honoring and revealing the remembrance of grande cycles and symbols to everyone along heshe's path, heshe hoped they could awaken them. Of course there would be jolting imbalances of the Enorganicots and Bvampiras, but heshe would do the best one could at diverting their vacuum of vulnerabilities… If they even could. The guardians even succumbed at times to their own dastardly, disequalizing pandemonia… yet, there was always a capability to learn and evolve. In and of itself, the Universo Divino would continue to become all possibilities at once. *Perhaps.*

Lolaboy fell into a deep dream. In the vision Lola was looking into a giant mirror. Heshe saw the image of a jaguar and Lola's own face. It was astonishing to see the beauty of one's true self. The marriage lived inside the seemingly contrary energies. Heshe saw how the characteristics could be united into harmonic balance.

"Oh well, aren't you the *serious* one! Who did your makeup, gurrrlll," shouted a weird-looking figure in a dazzling pink costume?!

It couldn't be… It was. "Jaguar Diva Queen," laughed Lolaboy!

"You thought it was *another* mirror? Hell no! Where's the cotton candy at this festival? Hmmm? I thought you were supposed to be riding on all those a… muse… mints…?" She grabbed Lolaboy and took them by the arm. "Come on! There's something those serious old biddy, witches left out! Good lord amighty, hell if I'd taken a journey with them, *I'd* be depressed!"

The two of them traveled. They approached the giant wheel that Lola remembered near the entrance to the Carnival. "Here, jump on, smoke a cigar, we're gonna have a good tyme!" She opened the door to one of the tin boxes that revolved around the enormous wheel.

Lolaboy jumped into the multi-colored car. Heshe watched as the entire Carnival of Souls came into view. They began to rise up as the wheel spun slowly. A strange man in a top hat played an organ and sang.

Rising up up up
Spit spat cat
Going down down down
Get that fat!
Spinning winning
Losing and boozing
It fits in a hat!
Winding and unraveling
Fortune and courtin'
Things that go bang
Fliberty jiberty jab
Off you go
Where it stops nobody knows!
Hehehehehehe hahahahahha
baahahahhahhhaaaaaaa....

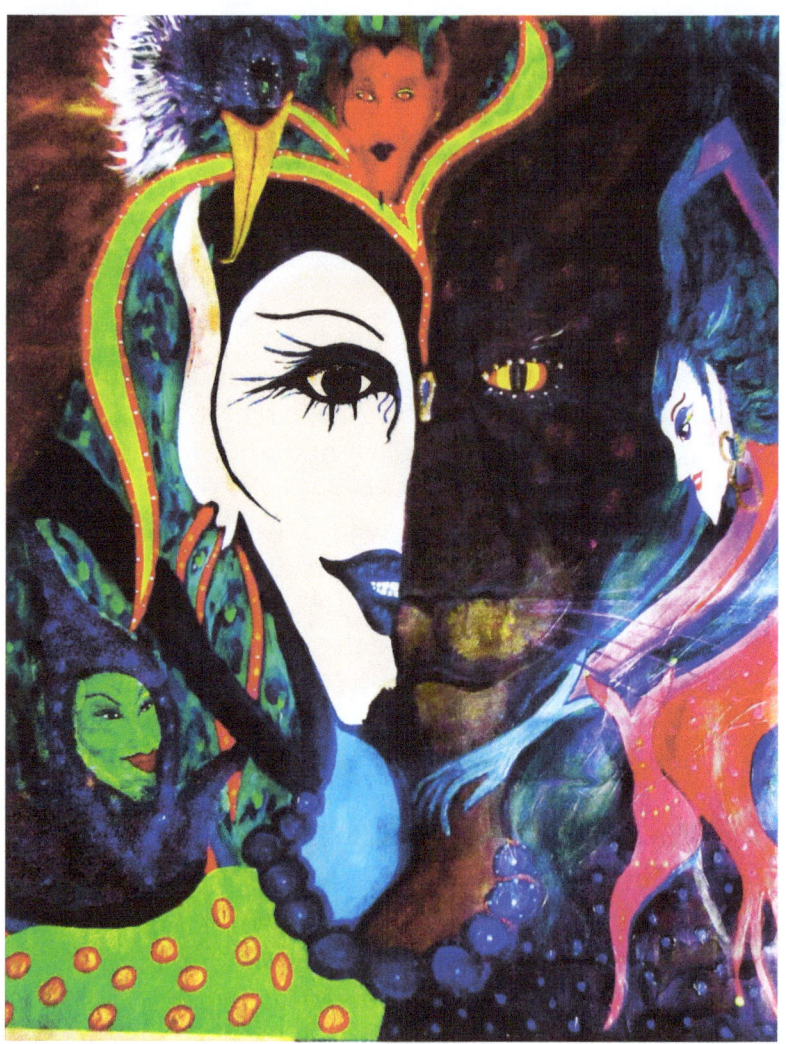

"Well good *lawd* a mighty! Listen to the old man croon like a bafoon," snickered Jaguar Diva Queen. "Now lookey here kid, anybody tell you about the fun? The amusing, pleasurable, sensual, entertaining part about the planeta? Eh?"

Jaguar Diva Queen crawled out of the car and hung from the side. The entire wheel wobbled a bit. "Can't this thing go any *faster*? Weeeeeeeeee weeee." She raised her hand and swirled it in the air and the giant circular device started to spin a lightening speed.

The jaguar magician gazed out the window one more time at the entire Carnival. Heshe saw the various gates clearly, the mirrors, the Krystal Village, the spheres, the sword, even the Urban Jungle off in the distance. There they were, all of them at their posts, Pumana Peakok, Nunki, Sera Pheam, Dusty Miller, even Banzeb stood at the helm of the matrix. What an astounding journey it had been through the maze to the center of the self.

"Ah, yes, the Planet of Great Consciousness indeed. Did anyone mention to you about the *chocolate cake*? Or, the cool music… the wild dances… the lusty romances…. Ba da da boom! Oh dear me, what a place that it is indeed. The views there are startling to some… *I* suppose." Jaguar Diva Queen reflected a bit. "I suppose it's like growing pains, sometimes kids gotta grow up, not to stop playing, but just do it all a bit more… a bit more *sassy*!"

"Look! There's Ocelotl and… I can't remember the other one's name… Ca… Ca… Calusaris! That's it. Can we invite them on board?" Heshe looked around, "What is this thing we're inside of anyway?" Lolaboy hung their head out the window and looked down; they were quite high in the air. Heshe felt as though they were in free-fall, completely airborne.

"Of course you're *flying*! Soaring in the bliss of knowing nothing about *everything*! Hah! This is the Cog of Chance, everyone has to ride this lil' ol', they call 'em *machines* on the planeta. Geez they went crazy with all the mechanismos down there. But, well, *hell*… who wouldn't? They tickle the illusion of transformation a bit. But you gotta be careful of getting addicted to those pickles." Jaguar Diva Queen opened her jacket and

c. huilo c.

184

out fell hundreds, thousands of mysterious looking gadgets of every shape, size and style.

"Whhaaat are *those*!" Lolaboy gleamed with delight as they gawked at the array of widgets falling from the pockets of Jaguar Diva. Voices began shouting from everywhere.

Without this you won't be able to
　　　　No words to express what it does
Not important how much energy
　　　　　　　　You need this
Do you want this
　　　　　　　　If you have this they will love you
　　My son of the stars you need it all
　　　　Perhaps there is no reason
Things things and more things
　　　　　　　Objects of every kind　Try them
　　　How much you'll love these
　Count them… thousands, millions, trillions
　　　　　　　　　Grains of sand

"Indeedy doo. They will *tantalize* you… *mesmerize* you until you fantasize you can't live *without* the thingamabobs, doohickies and thingamajigs! Well, maybe not *you* Lola, but *they* do! Poor bastards. Can't blame 'em. Problem is they have limited themselves. Ah, but that's *another* story. Hey, we're about to return to the landing pad. Betcha want the others to join us?" Jaguar Diva shook her arms and called out. "Hey you noodleheads get in one of these cars and ride with us to the starzzzzz!"

How bawdy Jaguar Diva was with her words. It seemed disrespectful.

"I *heard* that. Nah, I'm not discourteous just like to jest 'em a bit, or they take themselves tooooo serious and never have fun at all!" Diva swished her hand in the air again. "Now… Maxy, ain't he a doll… the operator? Can we get this old clunk to move faster than the speed of light? Hell, faster than any of us has experienced? Put the ole universo into high gear… test it? Eh? Um for the ol' diva?"

Within moments, the colossal wheel started to spin again and with each turn gained speed until it was moving so fast, the carnival became a blur. Then, a click and clack and the wheel broke off and raced into the sky. They flew. They flew far away. Further than any of them had been. After some time, the wheel slowed down and hovered in what appeared to be empty space.

"I don't know how you feel, but isn't it amazing? Hey Jaggy! Teach, you know where we are by chance?" Diva Queen stuck her head out of the car and looked around. Nothing, just pure darkness.

"As a matter of fact, I have a sense that we are in the abyssal plain. The Hoya Negra. Everything is birthed from here. Emptiness forms here into somethingness." Ocelotl smiled and took in a deep breath. "I suppose Benzab wanted Lolaboy to feel this place. It's quite a test of will to get here without the precise postures of trends. However, now that we are here… Lolaboy, you have *arrived*. To the place of all that ever was or will be."

Calusaris, who had been silent, suddenly spoke up. "The planeta, don't you think it and the entire Universo are a manifestation of sensuality? Of various forms and formulations of how things sense and respond and thus articulate the experience? All of it is in and of itself, *lustrous* beauty! Here we are in the realm of the matera negra, where some would say *nothing* exists. We exist and we are here! Even in the nothingness, something exists that allows it to be nothing, wouldn't you agree, Ocelotl?"

"Well said, and I'd like to offer that while there is the drive to develop, change, or come to know, there certainly are posits of incongruent behaviors that facilitate wary ways…"

"Listen to their ego-smeeeego dunder! Humanos have made us into relics and models of divino G-AWDS... They venerate us with shrines and even televisory programs that honestly beam nonsense into the lovely cosmos. Oh dear, how droll of me to even consider being worshiped." Jaguar Queen opened her jacket and took out some sort of globe on a stick. "They call this a sucker, candy, sweet. Mmmm…. It's probably one of the better inventions if you ask me. It tickles my tastebuds."

"Ocelotl. Jaguar, Calusaris. Thank you. I suppose in a way, the seriousness and the intensity is one side and the other, is like you say, Jaguar Diva, is to have fun, and to play? In retrospect, I *did* have fun. I am having a delightful time of discovery. It's the topsy turvy feelings I get sometimes that… well… disturb me."

"Well I'm sure they've got a pill on the planeta for that," baulked the Jaguar Diva! "Honestly, it's come to a point where I wonder if any of those humanos even feel anything… over steamulaated… Do they even feel any of the real stuff? You know…Ocey, the subtleties? The *sublime.* Purrrrr……"

"Well Lolaboy, those feelings are actually quite normal and eventually you reach a place where everything hums along effortlessly. The topsy turvy you speak of is the outcome of judgment, of whether this or that is good or bad. You are experiencing the quivering of opposition. Either way, this enables you to integrate into the holosphere of Gaia quite well. If you share empathy for the humanos in their wild transition, you can more easily let go and yield to the astonishing changes. You may reflect into their realm a posture of good will, harmony and even verve."

"Oh gawd yes. *Verve.* LOVE that word. Much better than nerve." Jaguar Diva gazed out into the distant blackness. "Oh dear! Look! It's… the *Phoenix.* I feel faint. Somebody have a glass of water? I just *love* that bird… I mean look at its feathers. Such plumage titillates my entire beingness. But, uh oh… You know when that bird's in the air…sumpin' big is about to happen…um hm."

"I called upon our dear friend. I thought it was time to advance Lolaboy to the trickster gates."

The enormous raptor came and clutched upon the giant ring, the Cog of Chance. It flew off with the lot and soon they were back to the Carnival of Souls.

They arrived back to amusements and it appeared the entire Carnival of Souls was having a party. Everywhere they saw beings of every kind dancing, singing, and hysterically laughing. The Keeper of the Masques was spinning hundreds of faces at the wondrous masquerade.

"Here! Here! Who is *who* after all? Which is a *witch* after all? Tut tut what is *what*? Why so?, said the sly?" The Keeper of the Masks bowed and escorted each of the partygoers through stately columns. "Nothing can be hidden anymore! Nothing at all! Reveal thyself, take off the masque, who *are you*? Who *am* I? A master in the game of polarity? Masking the adversary… only to see it was *myself*?"

One after one, the gatekeepers, the guardians, each of the guides encountered in the Carnival of Souls slipped through the noble posts. Lolaboy was bewildered as each one passed through the columns they became something *entirely* different. They converted into miraculous clusters of fractal particles and light forms.

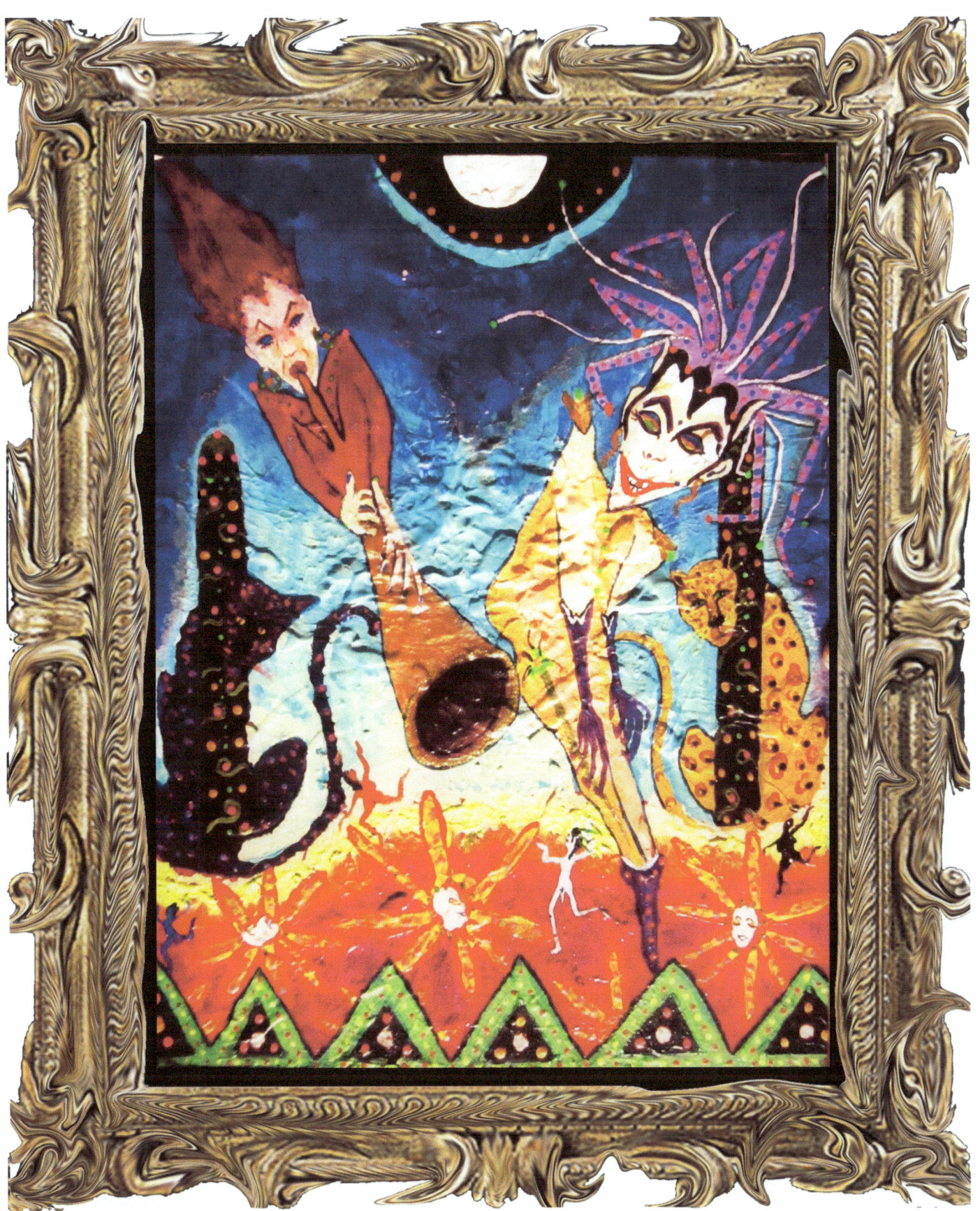

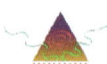

Mirror Mirror of us all!
You are a reflection of nothing at all!
Divine essence made of you?
Or, You made of Divine Essence?

The cosmic riddle!

Responsibility for it all
Use it if you wish
Accountability for the joy
Heaven and planet as one

The cosmic joke!

Look into the reflection
Vision of the future
Already enlightened
Humor thyself

The cosmic trick!

True to yourself
Knowing choice
Every situation is yours

The cosmic puzzle!

Survive, but why?
Your ability to exist
Quest to maintain

The cosmic conundrum!

Souls of the universe
Talismans for change
Collect your divinity

You are the cosmic mystery unfolding upon itself!

Jaguar Diva Queen and Jaguar Serpiente blew trumpets while La Cougera and Ocelotl stood solemnly next to the Pillars of Possibility. The Lunas suspended themselves gracefully above the pandemonium of the Carnival of Souls. The nights went on, and the days passed without notice as the festivities continued and they danced dusk to dawn, morning to night, until it became one mass, one source of opalescent holografica.

The feverish pitch echoed into the harmonies of the Universo. Moon Jaguars imprinted their will upon the divinity codigos. Wisdome and instinct gravitated towards a welcomed pattern that was in accordance to the sacred directive, the Decree of One.

In the midst of all the celebrating, stood Lolaboy, the one for whom the festivities had the most meaning. For it signaled the completion of the mission heshe had set out upon at the bequest of the moons. Ocelotl and La Cougera motioned Lolaboy to come to their side next to the Pillars of Possibility.

"Dear Lolaboy, spirited magician, it is now time. You have mastered the skills and talents of the various mirrors and gates well enough that we feel your path must take you now to the Planet of Great Consciousness." Ocelotl smiled warmly and put his arm around his friend, Lolaboy. "With your departure there is movement in the spiritus worlds, nothing has been taken for-granted about this masterful journey that you took for *all* of us." The master jaguar paused, "Thank you, Lolaboy.

Moreover, it is also the arrival of all that we wished for and more! Now off you go to integrate energy and reharmonize the various ways and patterns of the Universo. And, mostly, we hope that your efforts will magnify the willingness, the awakening and the magic of others in the double-spirit tribe to remember *who they are* and to quicken the new consciousness within Gaia's realm."

"Thank you dear teacher, I feel like an *entirely* new being. Well, of course I think of the innocence of the Selva and my time playing with all the creaturas there, and yet, also, I feel the pulse, the *quickening* in my blood to go out now…to live this calling that you and the creators engaged in me." Lolaboy turned to the columns that quivered like a mirage. "Am I to pass through this gate as well?"

"*Indeed*, Lolaboy, go beyond here… let the sum of all things become one again. It's a process of sealing the decrees and revelations you have acquired. These gates signify the wedding, the union of the selves, the principles and the subsequent harmony that evolves. On the other side awaits Loquatia, the Misstress of Mystiries. She will guide you to the realm of humanos with grace and ease so that you integrate the consciousness there effortlessly and sustain the vibrations attracted from this *adventurer's quest.*" La Cougera walked over to Lolaboy and took heshe's hand.

"We will escort you together to the posts, then walk through on your own accord. Now, Lolaboy, once on the planet, remember, their relationship with animals, trees, and rocks is of the objectified perspective, hence, their ability to communicate as you *will continue* to do so, has been jaded and even *completely* forgotten. Therefore, I will meet with you on the planeta, perhaps in humano, or at times, I may even be in the form of what they refer to you as a cat of the house."

"House cat," purred La Cougera. "*Some* of them do get treated very well. I hope that's where you land Ocelotl. Others bode more sadly wandering the streets at night eating trash."

"Very well then, I am ready." Lolaboy took Ocelotl and La Cougera's paws and walked forward to the Pillars of Possibility.

"One last thing. I think that it is wise for all of us to say, I am *Willing*, together." Ocelotl raised the paw with Lolaboy's hand, La Cougera the other. Together they roared into the pillars,

I AM WILLING!

Never had Lolaboy seen such a spectacular array of lights, beams, grids, colors, shapes, forms, patterns. Everything swirled, swooshed and twirled at a zealous pace. Heshe heard a voice chanting,

Into the ascendencia grid you flow
Activating the chakras you grow
Awakening the crystalline form you glow
Regenerating the story of one you flow

Oversoul of the eighths
Oversoul of the 144
Oversoul of the 72
Oversoul of the 3000

Master of the 12:12 lattice
Master of the 13:20 matrix

Entering the space again of all time and no time,
Forming the density of possibilities and tendencies
Let the intelligences witness each other again

Sound this tone into this magician
Will and spirit form to integrate the etheric cells
Body mass and lay lines congeal

Multiply, magnify, astound
Toned are the harmonies of the Universo
Multiplicity unified
Assimilate the benediction of the Jaguar Moons

Spinning molecular structures
Weaving the matera negra
A new template of opportunity

Rise now
INTO THE AURORA
Music of the spheres
Divino codigos

Permit this sacred union,
Allow this perfect harmony
Communicate the dance of harmony

INTO THE AURORA
Forgiveness
Regenerate, rejuvenate, resurrect
Absolute love

Enter this being, this vegetated mass of ecstatic amalgamation
Known to the Universo as LOLA

LOLA LOLA LOLA
Summoned by the masters themselves,
Awaken the matrices of chance
Sparked with joy, bliss and

The kiss of attraction

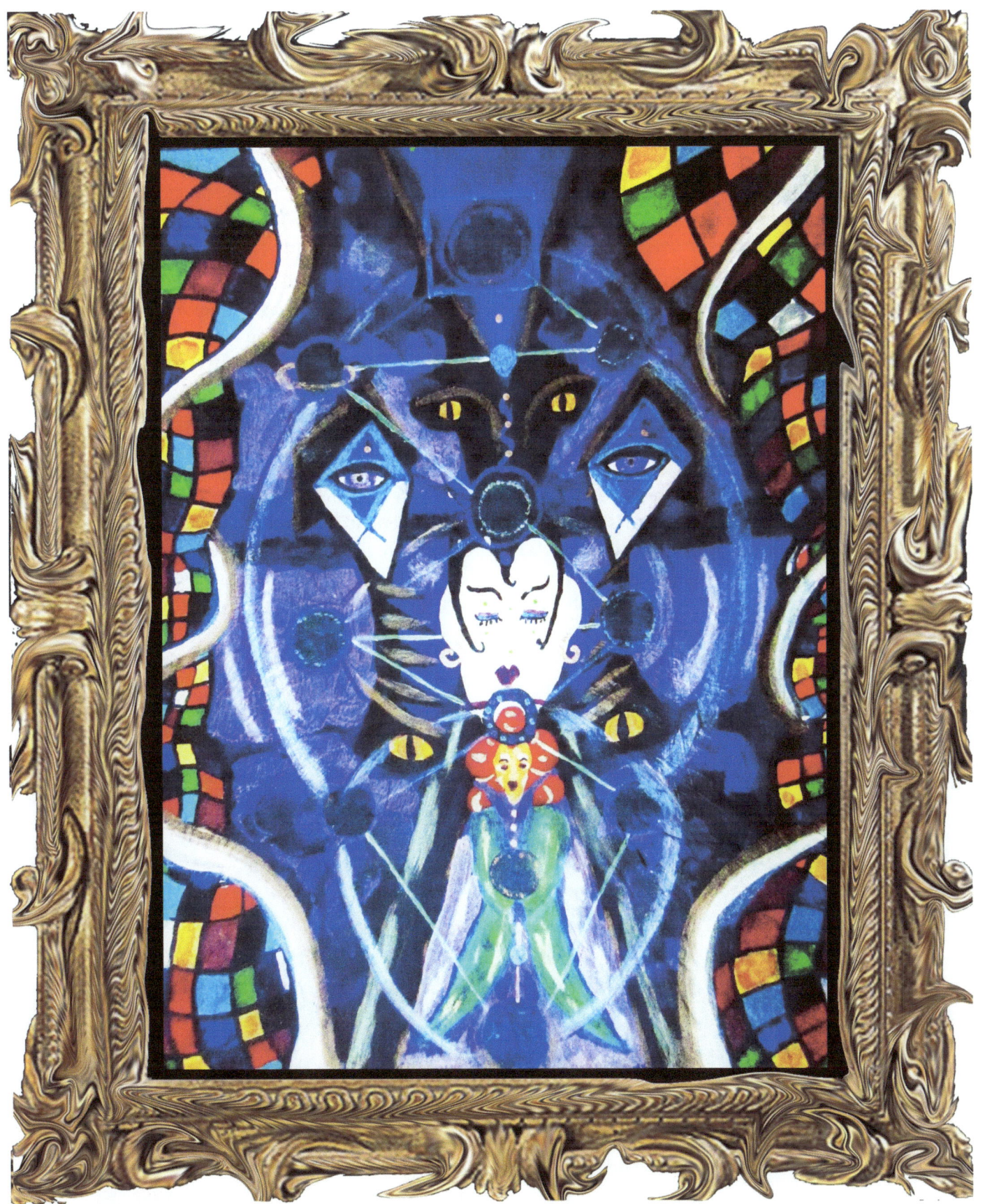

"Into the Planet of Great Consciousness, the Realm of Gaia and the tribe of Tellurusious, the humanos, we send you and invite you to explore the hearts of the bewildered forms. Take this wisdome of the gates and mirrors and reflect these truths into the holografica orb of consciousness."

Ashe! A ho! A lah! A ha! A lo ha! A mayne! For the benefit of all beings!
It is done! It is done! It is done!

Lola was free falling. Hovering in the absence of anything and the mesmerizing sequence of everything, Lola began to resonate to the tones of the humanos.

*W*hitelionmeetswhitebuffalowoman, Phoenix and Spiralus Serpiente gathered at the Entrada Da Finitum. They were waiting for the spirit of Lola to merge with the entire aspect ratios that Loquatia had summoned to solidify and seal the solemn promita of *Make ni Injurus* into the jaguar magician's Corazon Lattice. While they passed the time, they discussed the coming tides in the grande matrices of the Universo and Gaia's Realm.

"Certainly, these truths embodied in Lola will conspire and inspire others to mirror and reflect the pulse of truth into her orb. How could it not," commented Spiralus Serpiente?

With a deep sigh, Whitelion gazed upon the horizon. "Free will contains a possibility of passivity where choice is seduced by deluded appearances of deceit. Yet as I weigh the miraculous wonder of the existence of our ally, Lola, even now as I speak, there is a potency of many violent attractors in this realm of perception that echo of ancient future… with disastrous effects. When a sphere is presented at every level with choice, while the influences struggle, collapse and reform, with every perspective, option, belief system, attitude and fear, we must bear in mind that there exists the *possibility* humanos will not integrate the wonder and curiosity tones that Lola represents."

On the horizon, the *Entrada Da Finitum*, formed a huge eye. Phoenix called in the magic of the orbic field,

Ojo Siempretis Da Profundis Imaginus
From the base pyramid
Beaming the brilliance of emerald light

The place from which all existences share
Golden Phi frequency
Access to the divino origins

Cluster and open,
Blink and stare
Upon us in humor and humility

We beckon forth the dimensions
The admission into the adjacent lattices
Relative to this creation platform

Awaken Ojo Siempretis Da Profundis Imaginus
Rouse, stir, set off these uncanny and inexplicable whimsies
Sacred ellipsoid tone of the unknown!

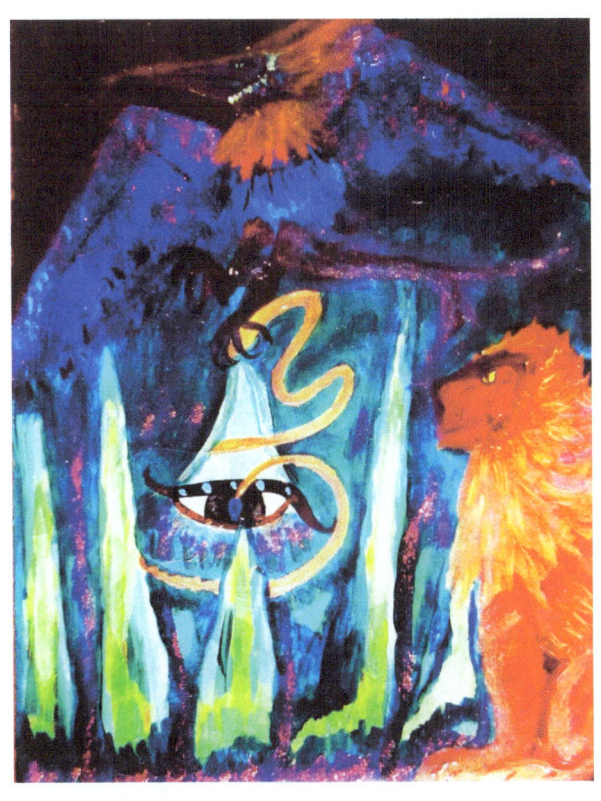

"Liberator of humanidad, summoner of truths, you have arrived!" roared the White Lion. "Now go into this… *uneasy* field. Indeed, for the benefit of all beings!"

The three masters, watched as Lola transformed into a beautiful jaguar magician and stood in the emerald light of the Ojo Siempretis. Slowly, hopefully, the Magus Jaguarus, of the Walks-betweens Querificus Androjananda Immaculus Gaeferundi, took a first step onto the Planet of Great Consciousness as a Keeper of the Golden Meme. Now, the quest, the sacred intent furthered itself into real time. The atmosphere quaked and quivered responding to the new presence. Wherever this wondrous container Lola wanders in the realm of Gaia, may it continue to bode good hope. Lola set out for a house in the distance where smoke rose from a chimney.

"I think I'll start there. It seems like a delightful abode." Lolaboy walked down a narrow dirt lane. "Who will be this first wondrous humano I shall meet? I call upon the Jaguar Magicians that lie dormant and hidden to feel my presence and come quick! Let us rise and weave the ecstatic union of the Moon and Jaguar into the realm of Gaia, for benefit of all beings!"

"*O*celotl, what is it that you dwell upon with your student? I sense an attachment. You *desire*?" Aguila Phoenis flapped her large wings as she flew next to the master jaguar racing through the forest.

Lithe and mysterious, the jaguar came to a halt beneath a densely foliaged canopy of trees. "Do you think the spirit, soulalma of Lola is fulfilled? The triggers we placed and pointed heshe too… I wonder of Lola's triumph in Gaia's realm. I would like to accompany heshe on this mission."

"The quandary of attachment, dear Ocelotl, even for you, is the *blindness* sometimes to observe it. For Lola to complete the cycle of the Moon Jaguar and transmute the veil of sinistro vibrato on the Planet, you know what must be done?"

"I do. Then soar above me as I travel alongside the magician, you cannot belittle my desire to assist. While my passion rises with a fervor like no other before, I aspire to be freed from manipulating the will within my former student."

Ocelotl knew that one of the traits within the jaguar tribe was a peculiar quality of connection… such passion that in itself could fall back into a paralysis and jeopardize the quest. Nevertheless the mission was ignited and the message now sounded into the furthest reaches and subterranos of the crystalline firmament. One could only ponder on the effect that this starseed would have upon the Planet of Great Consciousness.

Aguila Phoenis whistled a tune and took off flying alongside Ocelotl. The two would stay close to Lola, albeit, there were infinite possibilities of outcome and their presence would need to be transparent.

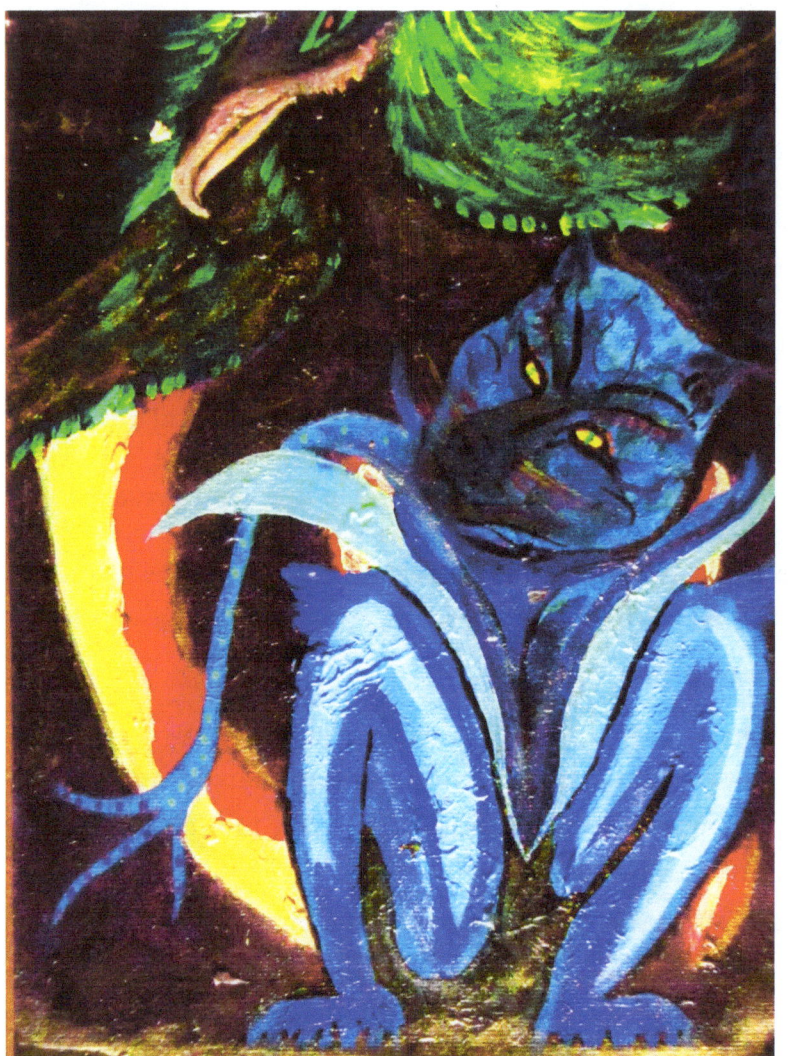

Procrastination, isolation prompt
Attachment, detachment, fracture
The will

Past things happen
New ideas form
Wonder suggests anew

Exhausted and discontented
Pollute the pollination
Of the latest vibration

Temptation to control
Prevent or exploit
A teacher must know
When to disengage and explore

The might of motivation
And allow it sail
Into territories uncharted

Navigate, translate, and aim
However, limits of expectation
Effortless and progressing

We await now,
The next story untold
The willingness unfolds…

c. huilo c.

194

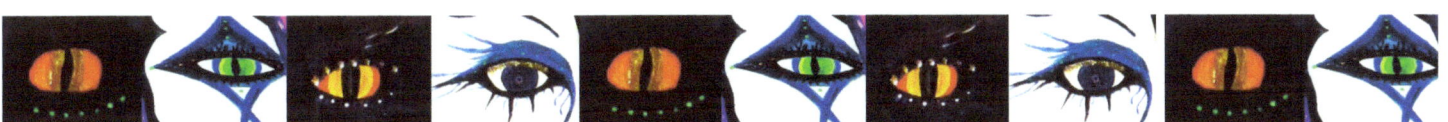

When Indians say that we are related to all things, we mean that all races have the same Mother, Mother Earth, and we are all brothers and sisters… If all things on earth are from Mother Earth, related through her, and sustained from her, there is no basis for prejudice.
--- Ed McGaa, Eagle Man, Mother Earth Spirituality

… they came to a place where they could see from above a line of light, straight as a column, extending right through the whole heaven and through the earth, in color resembling the rainbow, only brighter and purer… and there, in the midst of the light, they saw the ends of the chains of heaven let down from above: for this light is the belt of heaven, and holds together the circle of the universe…
--- Plato

By symbolically reflecting the soul's nature—the spiritual equality we share with all human beings—we can overcome cultural bias and religious prejudices and transcend physical gender differences and issues. Each soul is a spark of the Divine, is completely unique, and has the latent potential to originate in its expression of divinity.
--- from, Mandala, Luminous Symbols for Healing, Judith Cornell, Ph.D

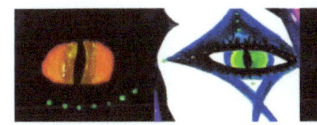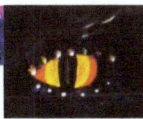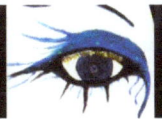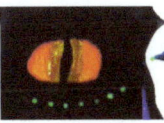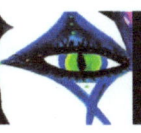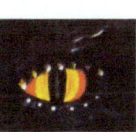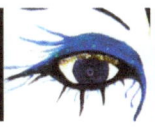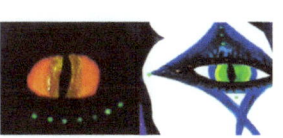

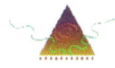

AFTERWARD

*T*ruly diving into the unknown, this set of tomes, *Marriage of the Moon and Jaguar*, surprised me. Like many immense creative projects, it seemed an ominous task. I wondered what would happen to Lolaboy if I let heshe "grow up". How do you encourage innocence to mature and yet allow the inherent good qualities to stay intact? As you have witnessed, this book became a study of mind-boggling, complex symbolism and metaphysical ideas.

And now, here we are in the year of 2012 and beyond. So much attention has been proposed about this particular period in human existence that it indeed has become a resonant tone for the entire universe as a planet struggles from blowing itself up or a species fights its own extinction.

I took the task upon writing the second book (which became two), with an attitude of complete openness, that is, let it become what it wanted and get out of the way. The way I manifested this work, was to dive in… completely surrender to the process. This was a style of free writing I learned from one of the multitude of writing classes I had taken during the 1990's. This method of writing is simply to keep writing the story until it is done…without looking back—except for brief reflection or to maintain an element of cohesion with characters and ideas. It was certainly very interesting and kept me fresh, inside it, in the moment. I disallowed the inner critic to obstruct the free will that wanted to participate along with a mass of amazing spirits that engaged my nimble fingers as they stroked the keyboard.

Many nights I would look at the 54 photos of the paintings and wonder, how could I describe them, what do they want me to say? Whilst I did have notions on the flow of a story while painting them, I finalized the sequential order of them just before undertaking the actual physical task of writing. I would simply look at a painting and then piece by piece see that they represented and aligned themselves to specific ideas.

The new characters were a delight to engage and create. Often, I was surprised by their names and qualities and sometimes shocked by their language. Getting into the groove of a particular character and having it be authentic with voice is challenging to say the least. If this book was to continue having the whimsy of the queer community, I wanted to invoke the camp, the humor, and the sense of being lost or left out from within the popular religions and governments of the modern world—and still continue to be fresh.

Moreover, as I finished it, like I feel with all art, just by its existence in physical form, there is now a vibration, a peculiar facet of consciousness that has now been refined and/or invited into life. And so it is done. 54 paintings and pages of magical invocations and ideas sent into the heart of human possibility. Whether the book reaches the numbers or brings in the critical acclaim, I understand that as an artist, I am devoted to making change through beauty. This is the lustrous beauty and whimsy that is so much fun that one cannot be repulsed or sent away, but instead come and "*join the circus*".

Of course, the ideas presented in this book are not new, although they are invited into this age as creatively as possible in a fresh way. The larger dream is to take these tomes and scatter their merriment onto a theatrical stage, or into an animated film. If you go back and read the story, and imagine the characters dancing in front of you on stage, or the paintings moving and oozing on the pages, you and I are on the same side of this mesmerizing possibility of fantasy, artist, principle and magic beyond our wildest imaginations.

Thank you to the hundreds of friends who supported the first book, *Flight of the Jaguar Magician*, even though they may have found the first book somewhat child-like for their tastes. Perhaps that is also part of this quest, to *invite* back in, the child of light that gleams and glitters from the eye of your essence self. Its embers are still glowing, and all you have to do is dive…into curiosity, wonder and allow your imagination to take you beyond the limited world of finite human passions and perception and fly with free will into the amazement of the infinite universe that surrounds us.